Orton Gillingham Workbook For Kids With Dyslexia

100 Orton Gillingham activities to improve writing and reading skills in children with dyslexia

BrainChild

Introduction

Orton-Gillingham is a structured, multisensory approach to teaching reading, used since the 1930s and proven to benefit all students, especially struggling readers. Neurologically and linguistically, it is the most frequent and successful model of reading intervention.

According to the National Institutes of Health, 95% of children who have trouble learning to read, reach grade level if they receive specialized help early on. Kindergarten through first grade is the "window of opportunity" to avoid long-term reading problems.

It is an individualized intervention for each child. It is flexible rather than preset, because it is based on a problem solving process. That process begins with identifying the child's learning disability. The next step is to develop a plan to address that difficulty.

An approach can offer more flexibility to meet complex needs than a program. However, because it is neither uniform nor preset, it cannot be studied with the same level of precision as a program.

That doesn't mean that an approach like OG isn't effective. Some programs based on OG principles have been studied and have reported good results. Teachers using an approach like OG must have in-depth knowledge in order to make decisions on a daily basis. They should also have a lot of experience implementing this approach with students who have diverse needs and ways of learning.

If you are familiar with OG, you may have also heard about Structured Literacy. This is an approach that The International Dyslexia Association defined several years ago. It includes six key elements of the language that the OG and other approches use.

A Structured Literacy approach includes teaching English sounds and their association with symbols. Each step must be taught explicitly. Teachers must guide students through the learning process to ensure that they have mastered important concepts.

Research shows that students with dyslexia benefit from instruction that have these elements. But as with OG, there is no specific research on that approach. Despite a lack of research, OG principles and methods are known to work. And teachers can tailor them to meet the specific needs of the student. In the end, what really matters is that the students receive instructions addressing their challenges.

In this book you will find activities based on the Orton Gillingham methodology that include...

- Letter knowledge
- Alphabetical order
- Sound Identification
- Rhyming words
- Sight words
- Homophones

Visit **www.BrainChildGrowth.com** and download 20 additional activities totally free.

LETTER KNOWLEDGE

Find and color.

A = pink ∀ = blue

a = red ɒ = yellow

A	∀	a	ɒ	∀	A
∀	a	A	∀	ɒ	∀
A	∀	∀	A	a	ɒ
A	ɒ	∀	a	A	A
a	A	ɒ	A	∀	A
A	ɒ	∀	a	ɒ	a
A	a	A	∀	∀	A

LETTER KNOWLEDGE

Find and color.

B = brown
ᗺ = green
b = purple
q = orange

B	ᗺ	b	q	ᗺ	B
q	b	B	q	ᗺ	q
B	ᗺ	ᗺ	b	b	q
b	ᗺ	ᗺ	b	B	B
B	b	q	B	ᗺ	b
B	q	ᗺ	B	q	b
B	b	B	ᗺ	ᗺ	b

LETTER KNOWLEDGE

Find and color.

C = red Ɔ = pink

c = green ɔ = blue

C	Ɔ	C	ɔ	ɔ	c
ɔ	C	c	ɔ	Ɔ	Ɔ
C	Ɔ	ɔ	c	c	Ɔ
C	ɔ	ɔ	C	C	c
c	c	Ɔ	c	Ɔ	c
C	ɔ	ɔ	C	ɔ	c
c	C	C	Ɔ	ɔ	c

LETTER KNOWLEDGE

Find and color.

D = purple ᗡ = green
d = orange p = pink

D	ᗡ	D	p	p	d
p	d	d	ᗡ	ᗡ	p
d	p	ᗡ	D	D	p
D	ᗡ	p	d	d	D
D	d	ᗡ	d	p	D
d	ᗡ	p	D	p	d
d	D	D	ᗡ	p	D

LETTER KNOWLEDGE

Find and color.

Ǝ = brown   Ǝ = green

e = purple   ə = orange

E	Ǝ	e	ə	Ǝ	E
Ǝ	e	E	Ǝ	ə	Ǝ
E	Ǝ	Ǝ	E	e	ə
E	ə	Ǝ	e	E	E
e	E	ə	E	Ǝ	E
E	ə	Ǝ	e	ə	e
E	e	E	Ǝ	Ǝ	E

LETTER KNOWLEDGE

Find and color.

F = pink Ⅎ = yellow
f = blue ɟ = orange

F	ɟ	f	ɟ	Ⅎ	F
Ⅎ	f	F	ɟ	Ⅎ	Ⅎ
f	ɟ	ɟ	F	f	Ⅎ
F	f	Ⅎ	F	ɟ	f
Ⅎ	f	ɟ	f	Ⅎ	F
f	ɟ	Ⅎ	F	ɟ	f
F	f	f	Ⅎ	Ⅎ	f

LETTER KNOWLEDGE

Find and color.

G = green Э = yellow
g = purple б = red

G	Э	g	б	Э	G
б	g	g	Э	G	б
G	б	Э	G	g	Э
G	g	б	g	Э	G
Э	G	Э	g	б	g
G	б	б	G	Э	g
g	g	G	б	б	G

LETTER KNOWLEDGE

Find and color.

H = pink
I = orange
h = green
ч = red

h	ч	I	H	ч	I
I	h	h	ч	h	H
h	ч	I	H	h	ч
h	H	H	h	ч	h
H	h	ч	I	ч	h
h	I	ч	h	ч	h
H	h	h	ч	ч	I

LETTER KNOWLEDGE

Find and color.

I = pink ⊢⊣ = orange
i = green ! = red

i	!	⊢⊣	I	!	⊢⊣
⊢⊣	i	I	!	i	!
i	!	⊢⊣	I	I	!
i	I	!	i	!	i
I	i	!	⊢⊣	!	i
i	⊢⊣	!	i	!	I
I	i	i	!	!	⊢⊣

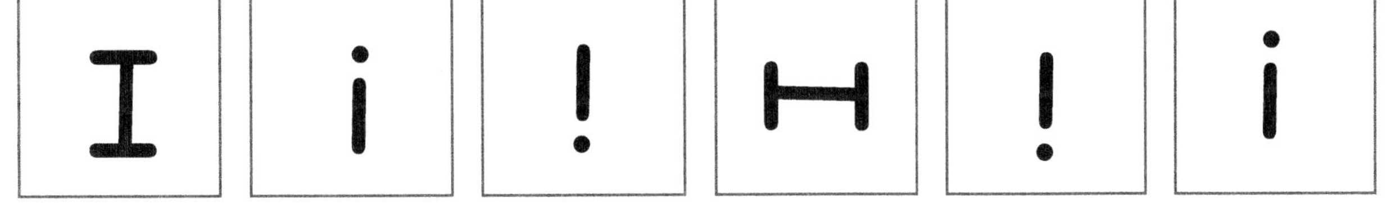

LETTER KNOWLEDGE

Find and color.

J = pink
j = green
ſ = orange
ɾ = red

j	ſ	J	ɾ	ſ	j
ſ	j	J	ſ	J	ſ
j	ɾ	ɾ	J	J	ſ
j	j	ſ	J	ɾ	J
ſ	j	ſ	J	ɾ	j
j	ɾ	ſ	J	ɾ	j
J	j	J	ɾ	ſ	J

LETTER KNOLWEDGE

Find and color.

K = pink
k = red
K = blue
ʞ = yellow

K	ꓘ	k	ʞ	ꓘ	K
ꓘ	k	K	ꓘ	ʞ	ʞ
K	ꓘ	ʞ	k	K	ꓘ
K	ʞ	ʞ	K	k	k
k	k	ʞ	k	ꓘ	K
K	ʞ	ꓘ	k	ʞ	k
K	k	k	ʞ	ʞ	K

LETTER KNOLWEDGE

Find and color.

ㄴ = brown
ㅣ = purple
ㄱ = green
ㅡ = orange

ㄴ	ㄱ	ㅣ	ㅡ	ㄱ	ㄴ
ㅣ	ㅡ	ㄴ	ㅣ	ㄱ	ㄱ
ㄴ	ㄱ	ㅣ	ㄴ	ㄴ	ㅡ
ㅣ	ㄱ	ㄱ	ㅣ	ㅡ	ㄴ
ㄴ	ㅡ	ㅣ	ㄴ	ㄱ	ㅡ
ㄴ	ㄱ	ㄱ	ㄴ	ㅣ	ㅣ
ㅡ	ㅣ	ㄴ	ㄱ	ㄱ	ㅣ

LETTER KNOLWEDGE

Find and color.

M = red W = pink
m = green ɯ = blue

M	W	M	ɯ	ɯ	M
ɯ	M	m	ɯ	m	m
M	W	ɯ	m	m	W
M	ɯ	m	M	M	m
m	M	W	m	ɯ	m
M	W	ɯ	M	ɯ	m
m	M	m	W	ɯ	m

LETTER KNOLWEDGE

Find and color.

N = purple И = green
n = orange u = pink

N	И	N	u	u	n
u	n	n	N	И	u
n	u	И	n	N	u
И	N	u	n	N	n
n	N	И	n	u	И
n	u	u	N	u	N
n	И	N	u	И	n

LETTER KNOLWEDGE

Find and color.

O = brown O = green
o = purple o = orange

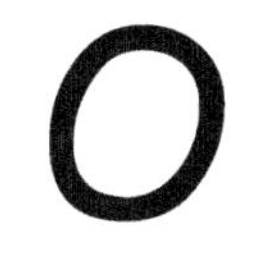

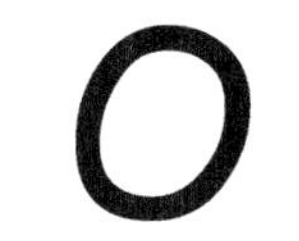

LETTER KNOLWEDGE

Find and color.

P = pink d = yellow

p = blue d = orange

P	d	P	d	d	P
d	p	P	d	d	d
p	d	d	P	P	d
P	p	d	P	d	p
d	p	d	p	d	P
p	d	d	P	d	p
p	p	p	d	d	P

LETTER KNOLWEDGE

Find and color.

Q = green   Ø = yellow
q = purple   b = red

Q	Ø	q	b	Ø	Q
b	Q	q	Ø	Q	b
Q	b	Ø	Q	q	Ø
q	Q	q	Q	b	Q
b	q	Ø	Q	Ø	Q
Q	b	q	Q	b	Q
q	q	Q	q	b	q

LETTER KNOLWEDGE

Find and color.

R = pink ꓤ = orange

r = green ɹ = red

R	ɹ	r	ꓤ	ꓤ	R
ɹ	r	r	ꓤ	R	ɹ
R	ɹ	ꓤ	R	r	ꓤ
r	R	ɹ	r	ꓤ	R
ꓤ	r	ꓤ	R	ɹ	r
R	ɹ	ꓤ	R	ɹ	R
r	R	r	ꓤ	ɹ	r

LETTER KNOLWEDGE

Find and color.

S = pink S = orange

s = green s = red

S	s	S	s	S	s
s	S	s	S	s	S
S	s	S	S	s	s
S	S	s	s	S	s
S	s	S	s	s	S
s	s	s	S	S	s
S	s	S	s	s	S

LETTER KNOLWEDGE

Find and color.

T = pink ⊥ = orange

† = green + = red

T	⊥	†	⊥	+	T
⊥	†	†	⊥	T	+
†	⊥	⊥	T	†	+
T	 †	 +	†	⊥	†
+	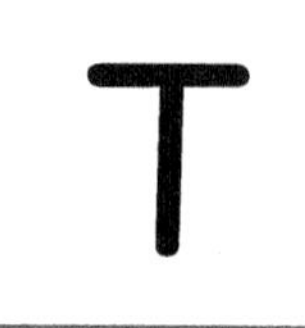 T	 ⊥	 †	 +	T
T	 +	 ⊥	 †	 ⊥	 †
 †	T	T	+	⊥	 †

LETTER KNOWLEDGE

Find and color.

U = pink
u = red
∩ = blue
n = yellow

U	∩	u	n	∩	U
∩	u	U	∩	n	∩
U	n	∩	U	u	n
u	n	∩	u	U	U
u	u	n	U	n	u
u	n	∩	u	∩	u
U	u	u	∩	∩	u

LETTER KNOWLEDGE

Find and color.

V = brown   Λ = green

v = purple   ʌ = orange

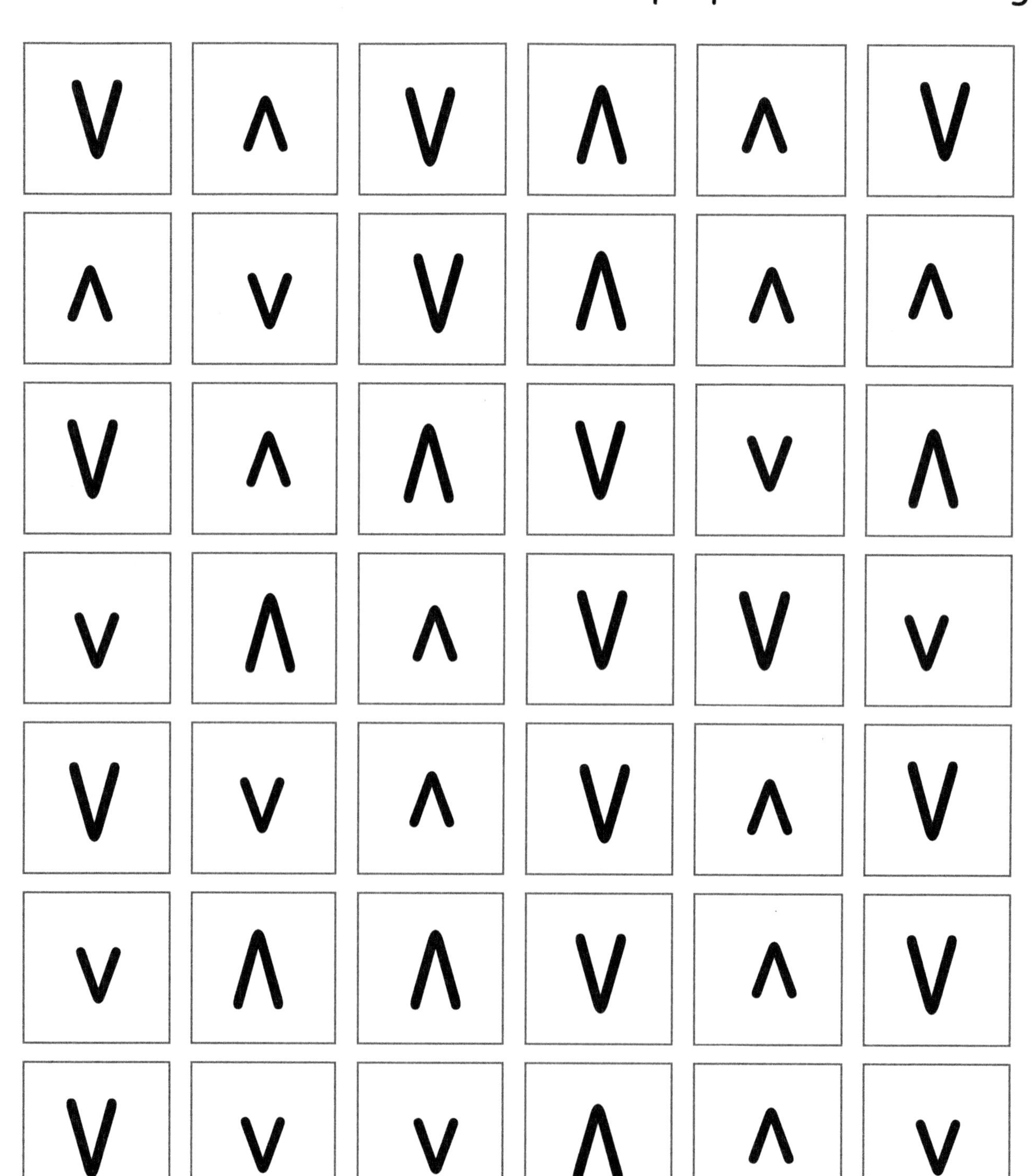

LETTER KNOWLEDGE

Find and color.

W = red M = pink

w = green m = blue

			m		M

w					

	m				
	m		m	w	m

LETTER KNOWLEDGE

Find and color.

X = purple ✕ = green
x = orange × = pink

	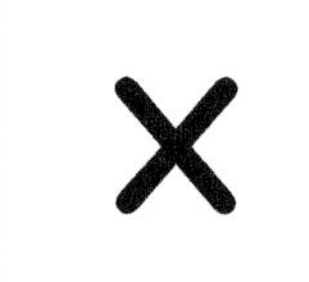				

LETTER KNOWLEDGE

Find and color.

y = brown | ʎ = green
y = purple | ʎ = orange

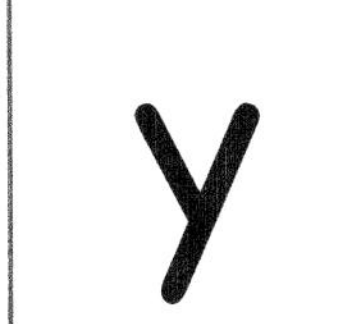	ʎ				
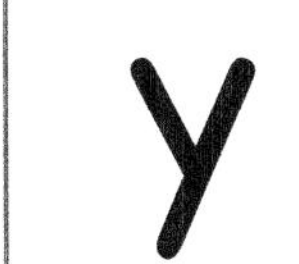			ʎ	ʎ	y

LETTER KNOWLEDGE

Find and color.

Z = pink
z = blue
N = yellow
ɴ = orange

Z	z	N	Z	ɴ	z
Z	Z	z	z	ɴ	z
N	z	N	N	z	z
Z	N	z	ɴ	Z	Z
ɴ	Z	z	Z	ɴ	z
Z	ɴ	Z	ɴ	z	Z
z	Z	N	z	ɴ	N

ABC ORDER

Read the words and write them in alphabetical order.

Words	Order
sun	1.
rain	2.
dig	3.
map	4.
flower	5.
pet	6.
nest	7.
cap	8.
log	9.
garden	10.

ABC ORDER

Read the words in each row. Write them in alphabetical order.

egg rat ant bed

1.	2.	3.	4.

bird wolf jug top

1.	2.	3.	4.

hill pen mug net

1.	2.	3.	4.

hot tub zoo ox

1.	2.	3.	4.

ABC ORDER

Look at the pictures. Write their names in alphabetical order.

1.

2.

3.

4.

5.

6.

7.

8.

ABC ORDER

Circle the word that comes FIRST in alphabetical order in each row.

hill	fresh	tall	pig
fine	smell	drop	kite
add	card	happy	new
this	odd	map	fin
pony	van	urn	joke
sun	yolk	quail	rat
hut	duck	lion	west

ABC ORDER

Read the words. Write the words in ABC order.

sit 1.________
fan 2.________
pat 3.________
dig 4.________

pig 1.________
hug 2.________
man 3.________
bit 4.________

gut 1.________
bag 2.________
van 3.________
ant 4.________

cat 1.________
log 2.________
jug 3.________
fan 4.________

ABC ORDER

Read the words and write them in alphabetical order.

face	baby	like	rabbit
parrot	jackal	wheel	house
	under	owl	

1. ____________________

2. ____________________

3. ____________________

4. ____________________

5. ____________________

6. ____________________

7. ____________________

8. ____________________

9. ____________________

10. ____________________

BEGINNING SOUNDS

Look at the pictures. Circle the correct beginning sound.

c t g

b s e

d c o

m r l

v q b

f j l

a h p

u r k

i o s

BEGINNING SOUNDS

Shade the beginning sound of each picture.

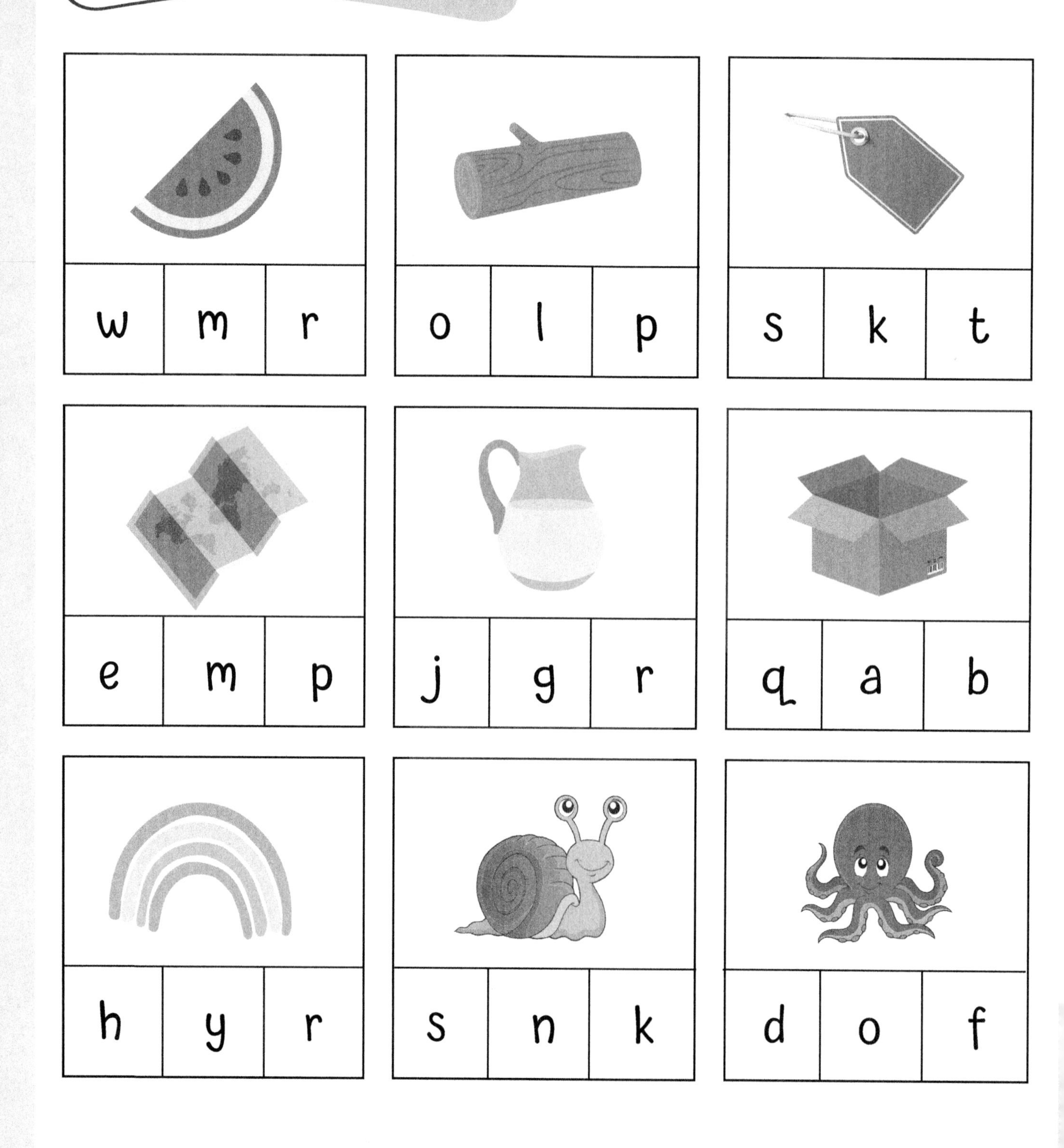

BEGINNING SOUNDS

Write the beginning sound for each picture in the given box.

BEGINNING SOUNDS

Color the circle with the correct beginning sound for each picture.

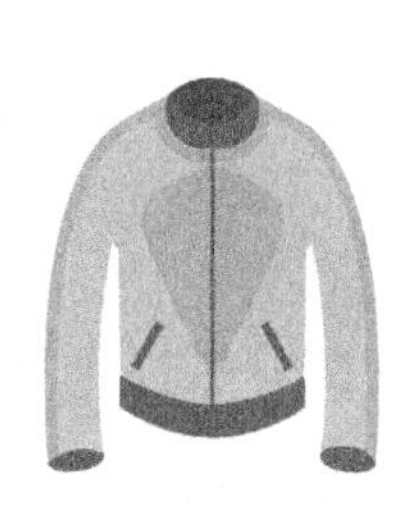

k m

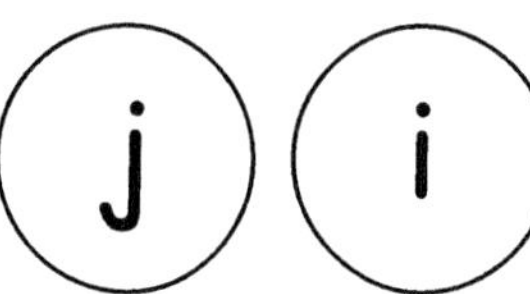

a k

p s

n r

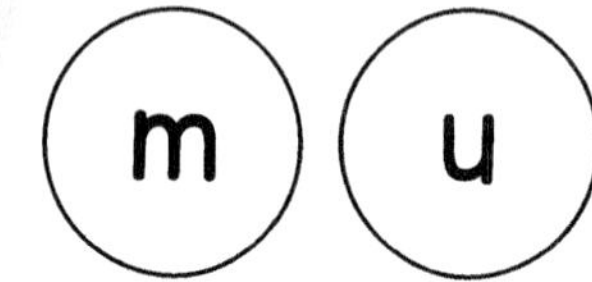

l i

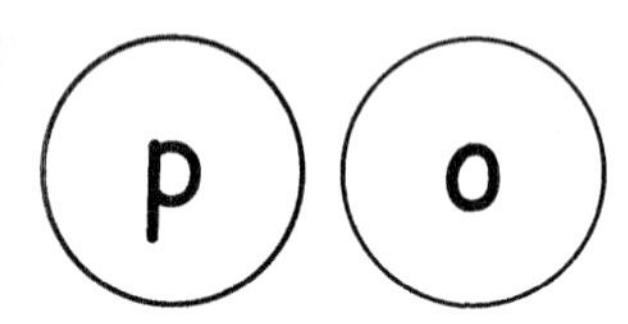

u h

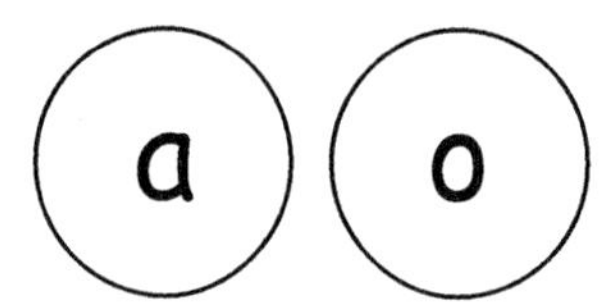

s f

r y

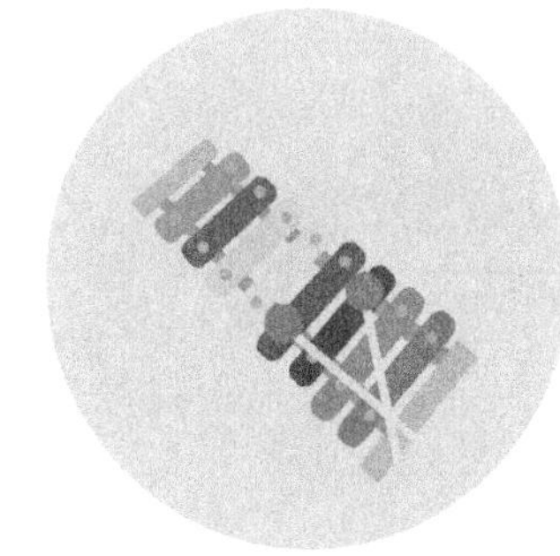

x n

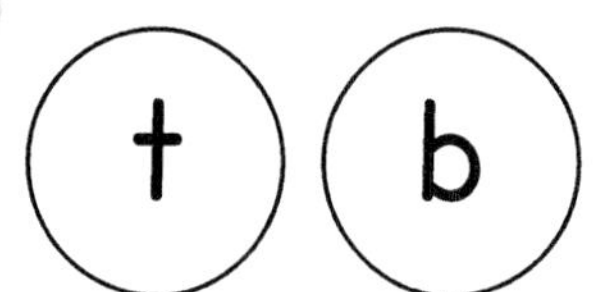

v z

m u

BEGINNING SOUNDS

Write the beginning sound for each picture.

BEGINNING SOUNDS

Say the name of each picture out loud. Circle the correct beginning sound for the picture in each row.

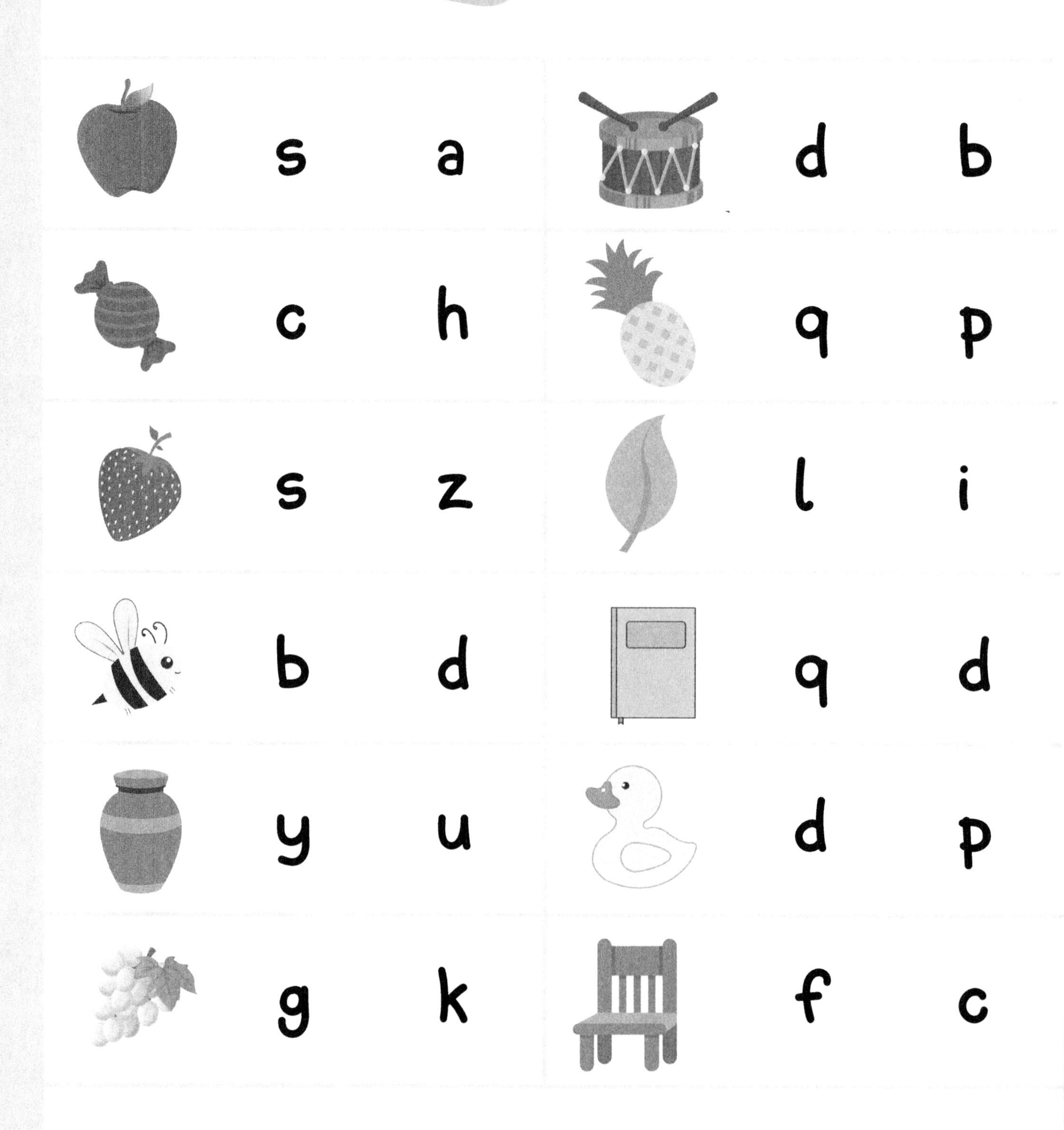

BEGINNING SOUNDS

Trace the correct beginning sound with the color RED.

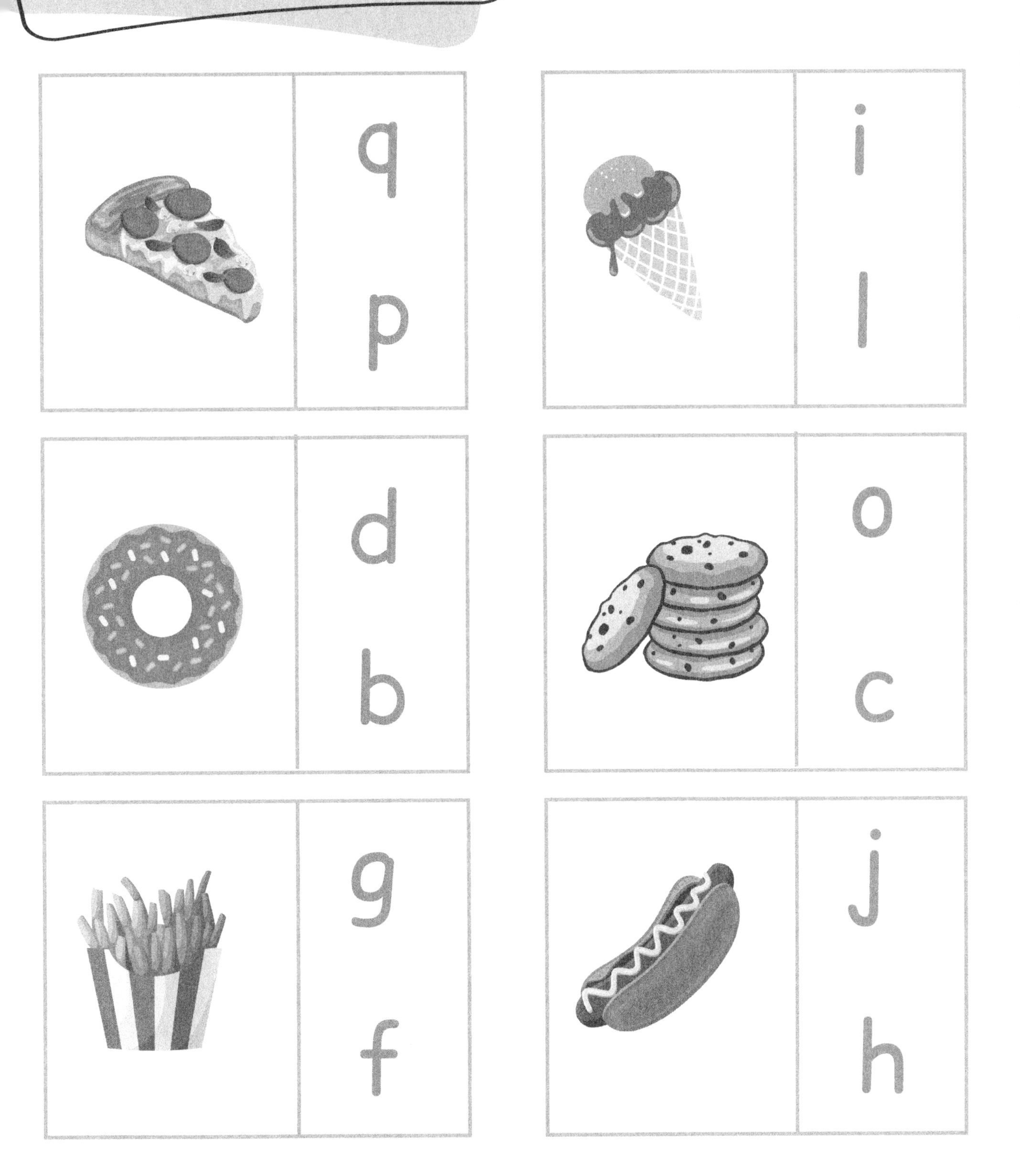

BEGINNING SOUNDS

Look at the pictures. Write the correct beginning sound below the picture.

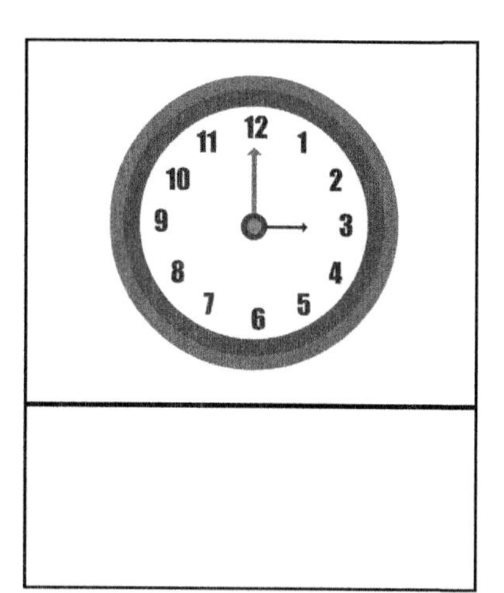

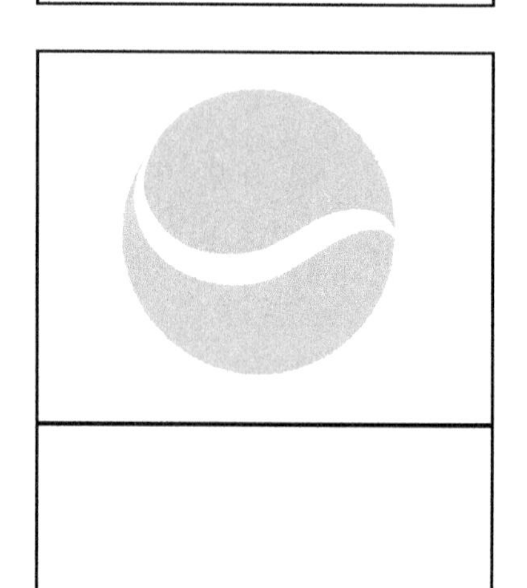

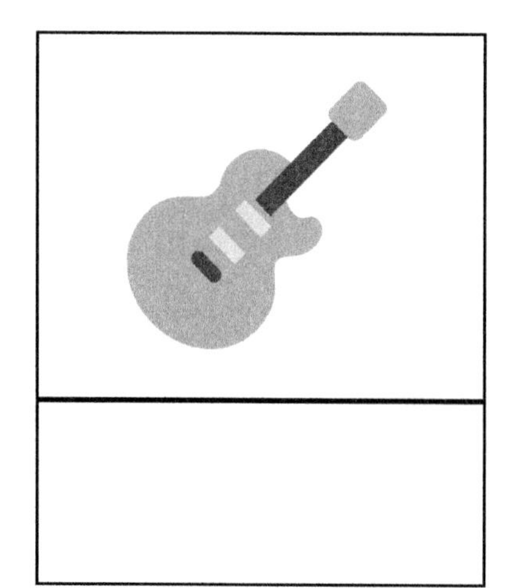

ENDING SOUNDS

Look at the pictures. Write the correct ending sound.

va ___

an ___

plan ___

sta ___

bu ___

shar ___

fo ___

clou ___

boo ___

ENDING SOUNDS

Look at the pictures. Circle the correct ending sound.

c t g

b s e

d s o

m r l

k q b

f j n

t h p

u r k

i m s

ENDING SOUNDS

Say the name of each picture out loud. Write the correct ending sound of each picture.

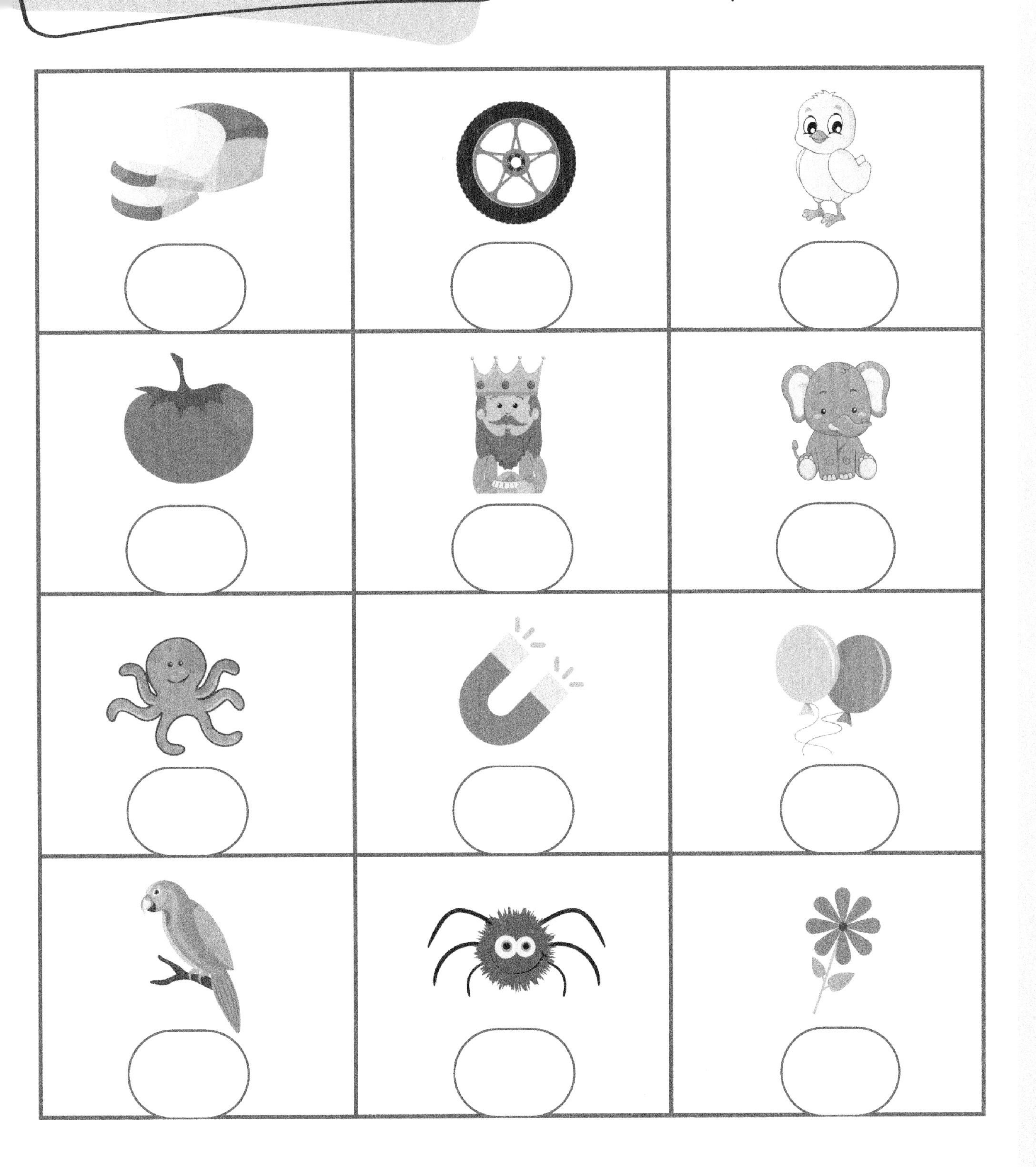

ENDING SOUNDS

Say the name of each picture out loud. Shade the correct ending sound of each picture.

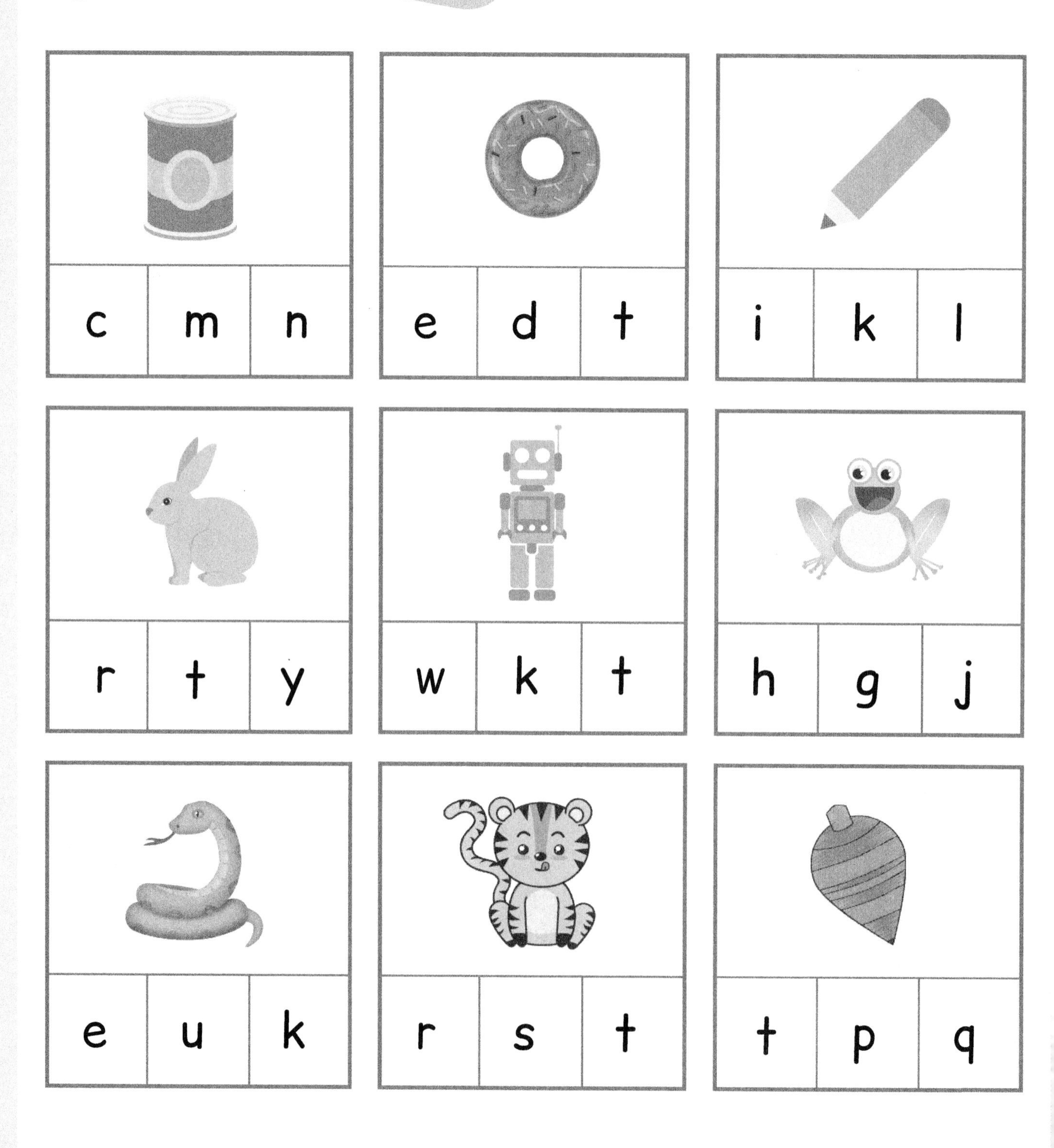

ENDING SOUNDS

Look at the pictures. Color the box with the correct ending sound.

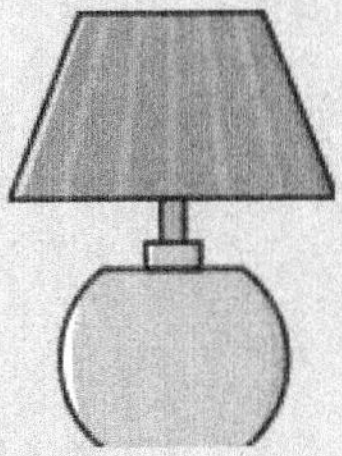

a	m
p	l

j	o
g	p

i	l
a	n

d	b
p	q

h	f
n	o

y	t
h	u

e	b
d	p

c	m
b	d

ENDING SOUNDS

Look at the pictures. Write the ending sound for each picture.

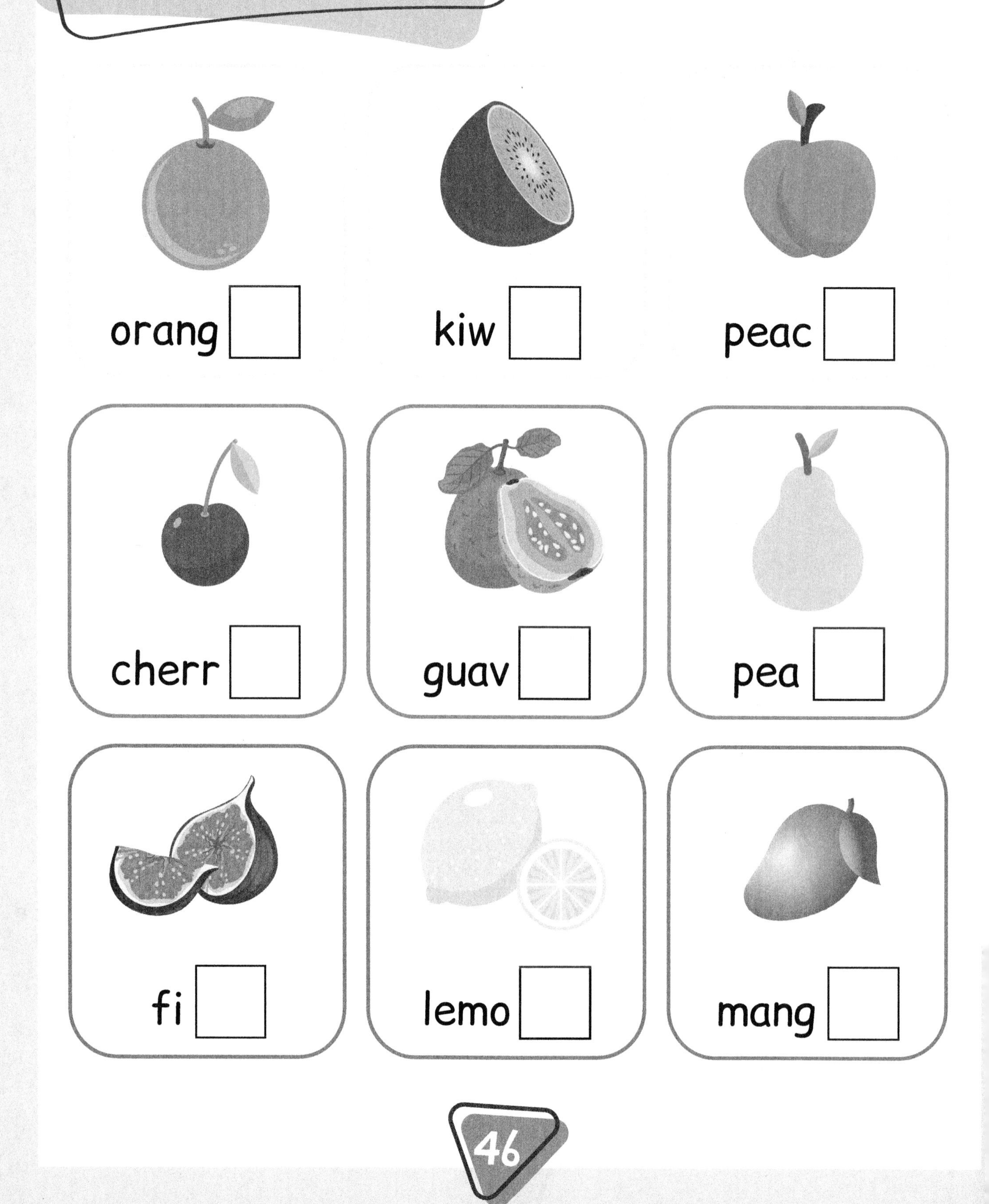

ENDING SOUNDS

Look at the pictures. Trace the correct ending sound with the color BLUE.

ENDING SOUNDS

Say the name of each picture out loud. Write the ending sound for each picture below.

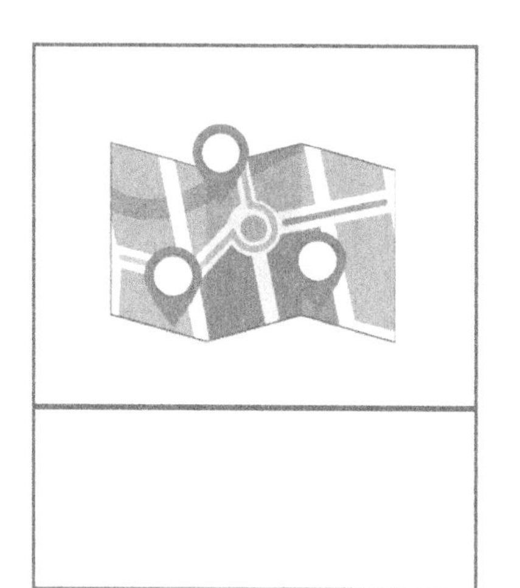

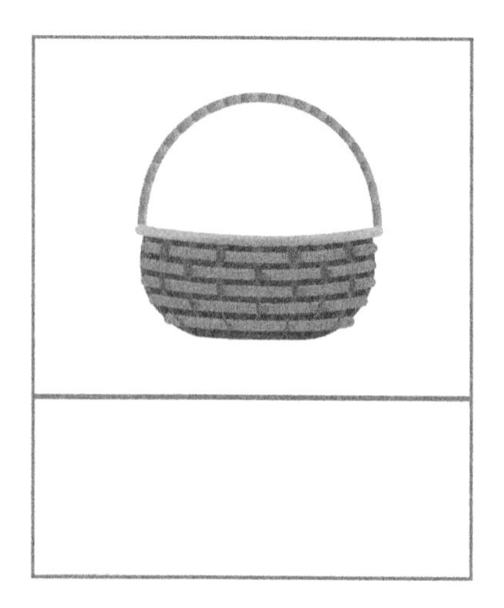

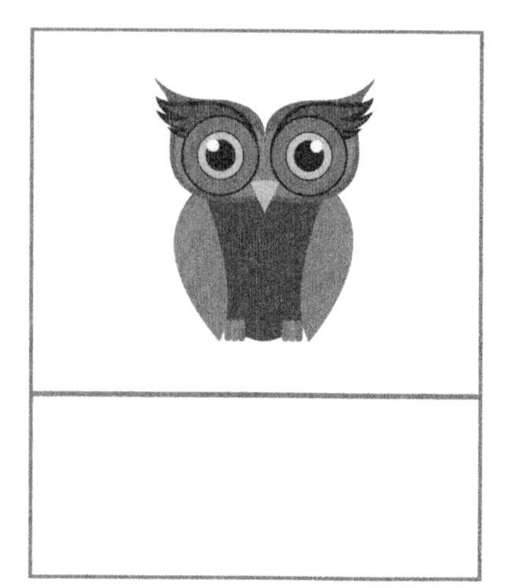

ENDING SOUNDS

Draw a line to match the pictures with their ending sounds.

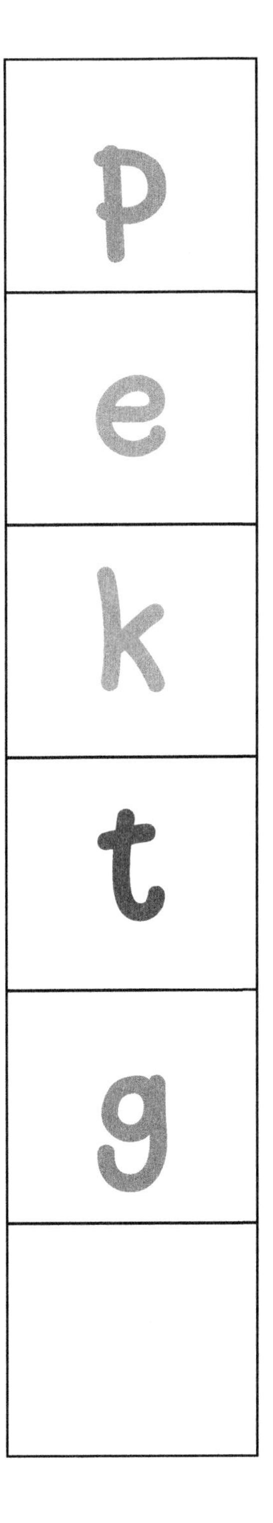

ENDING SOUNDS

Write the ending sound of each picture in the box.

s	a	

c	u	

b	u	

r	u	

h	u	

e	a	

d	o	

s	u	

r	a	

a	n	

f	o	

i	c	

RHYMING WORDS

Read the words. Circle the words that rhyme with the word on the left side.

map	cap	top	lap
tin	bun	bin	gun
ten	pen	nun	men
rag	mug	bag	dog
sun	nun	bun	man
frog	log	fog	big

RHYMING WORDS

Draw a line to match the pictures whose names rhyme with each other.

 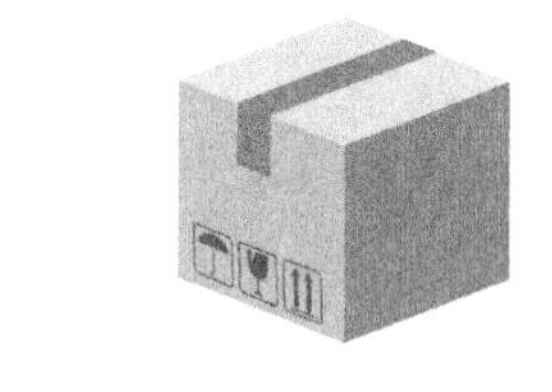

 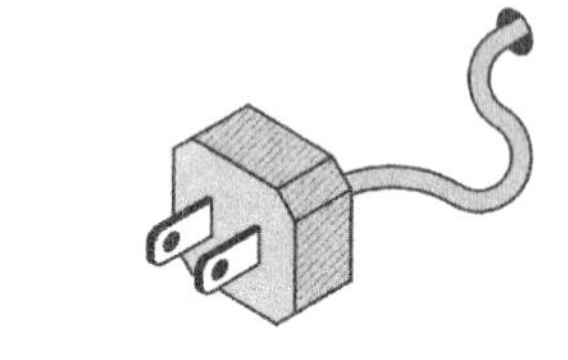

RHYMING WORDS

Identify the name of the picture. Circle the words that rhyme with the picture.

	light	loud	crowd
	gate	kite	mate
	pin	pig	rag
	net	met	fed
	barn	born	ran
	king	zone	ping

RHYMING WORDS

Identify the name of the picture. Circle the correct word that rhymes with the picture.

see bat	pin fox	sun bag
pin pet	ram map	bake bike
cut pat	cap sip	fog fig
tie lift	hike bite	man jam

RHYMING WORDS

Read the words and circle the word that does not rhyme with the others in each row.

feet meat light heat

cone tune tone bone

map pat lap cap

pin tin bun bin

let bed fed led

hot pit lot not

cow pow can row

RHYMING WORDS

Draw a line to match the words that rhyme with each other.

lame	boat
cane	sheep
van	locket
jump	fame
pocket	ban
deep	lane
coat	pump

RHYMING WORDS

How many rhymes can you think of for each word? Write them.

fan	
plane	
snail	
ice	
game	
book	
tree	

RHYMING WORDS

How many rhymes can you think of for each word? Write them.

RHYMING WORDS

Say the name of each picture out loud. Write the word next to each picture that rhymes.

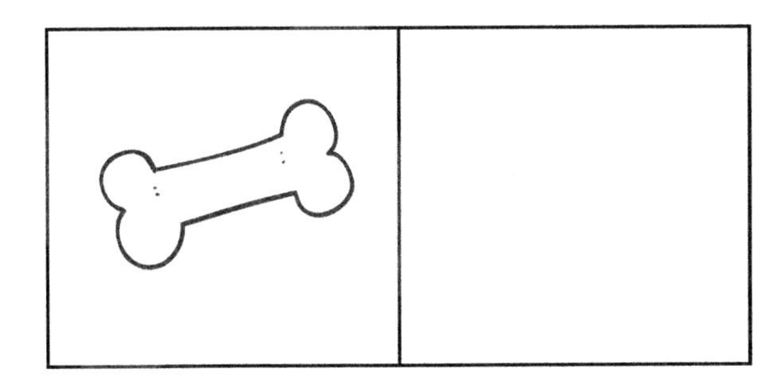

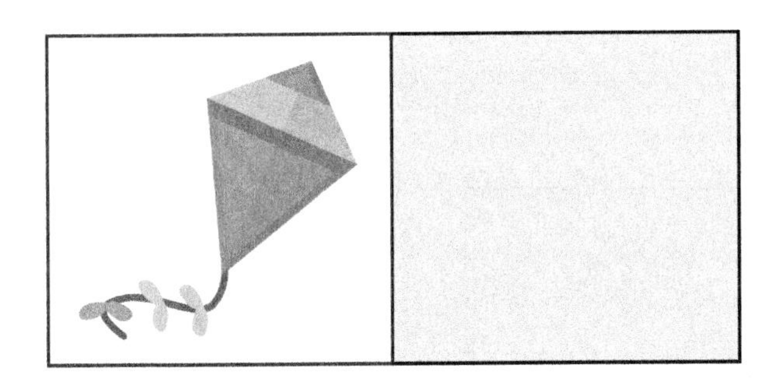

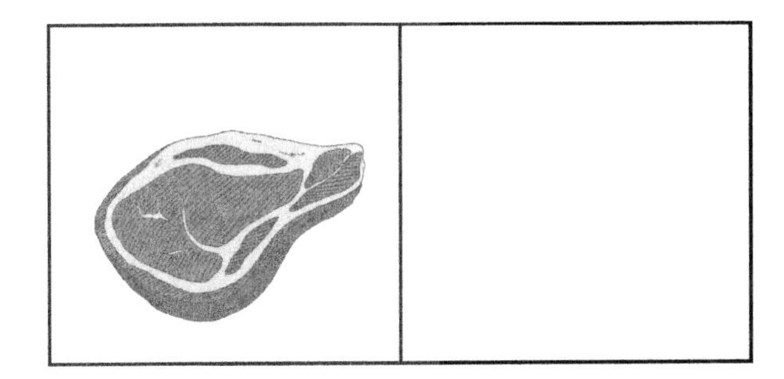

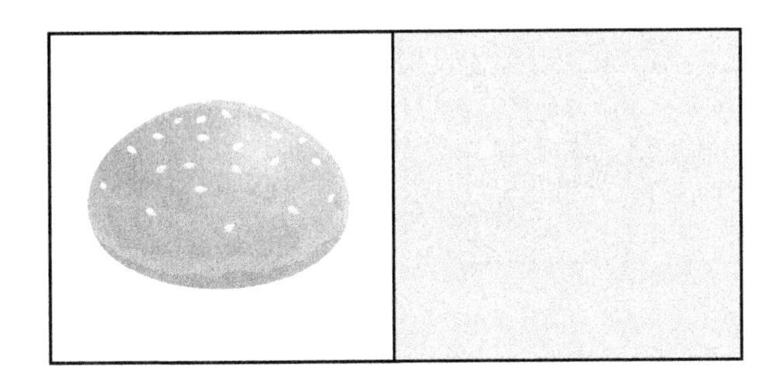

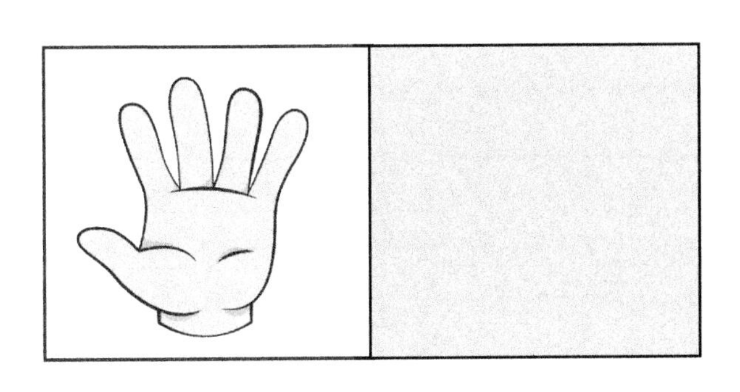

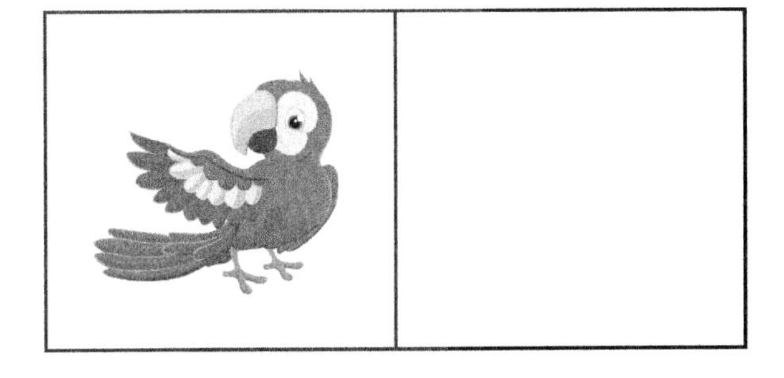

RHYMING WORDS

Color the words that rhyme with each other in every row. Use different colors for each row.

face	race	bake	trace
mole	ball	hole	bell
cook	look	fake	book
seed	fade	feed	weed
care	gave	cave	save
jump	stay	pale	hay

BLENDING SOUNDS

Say the name of each picture. Circle the correct blending sound for each picture.

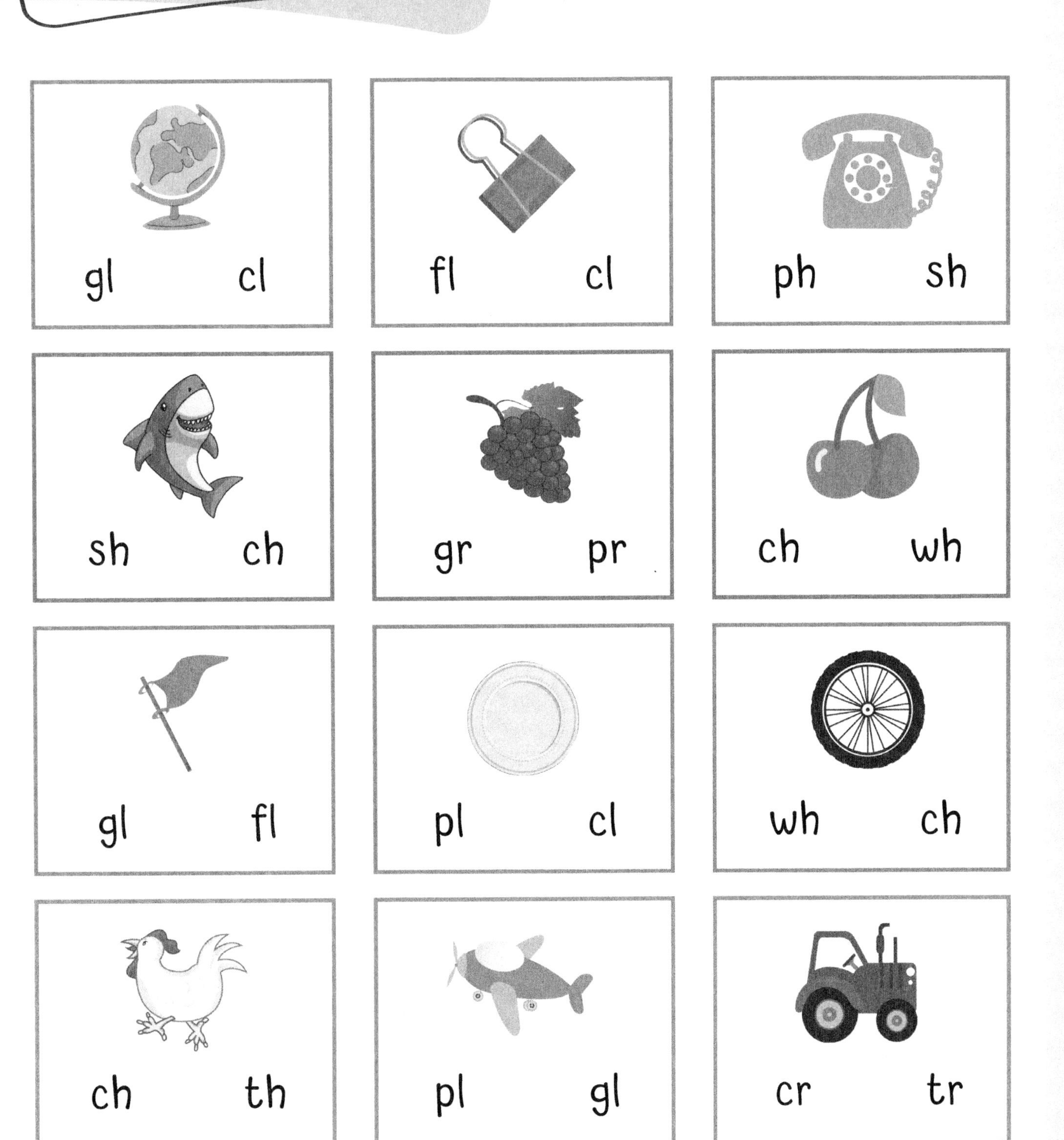

BLENDING SOUNDS

Look at the pictures. Write the correct blending sounds for each picture to finish the word.

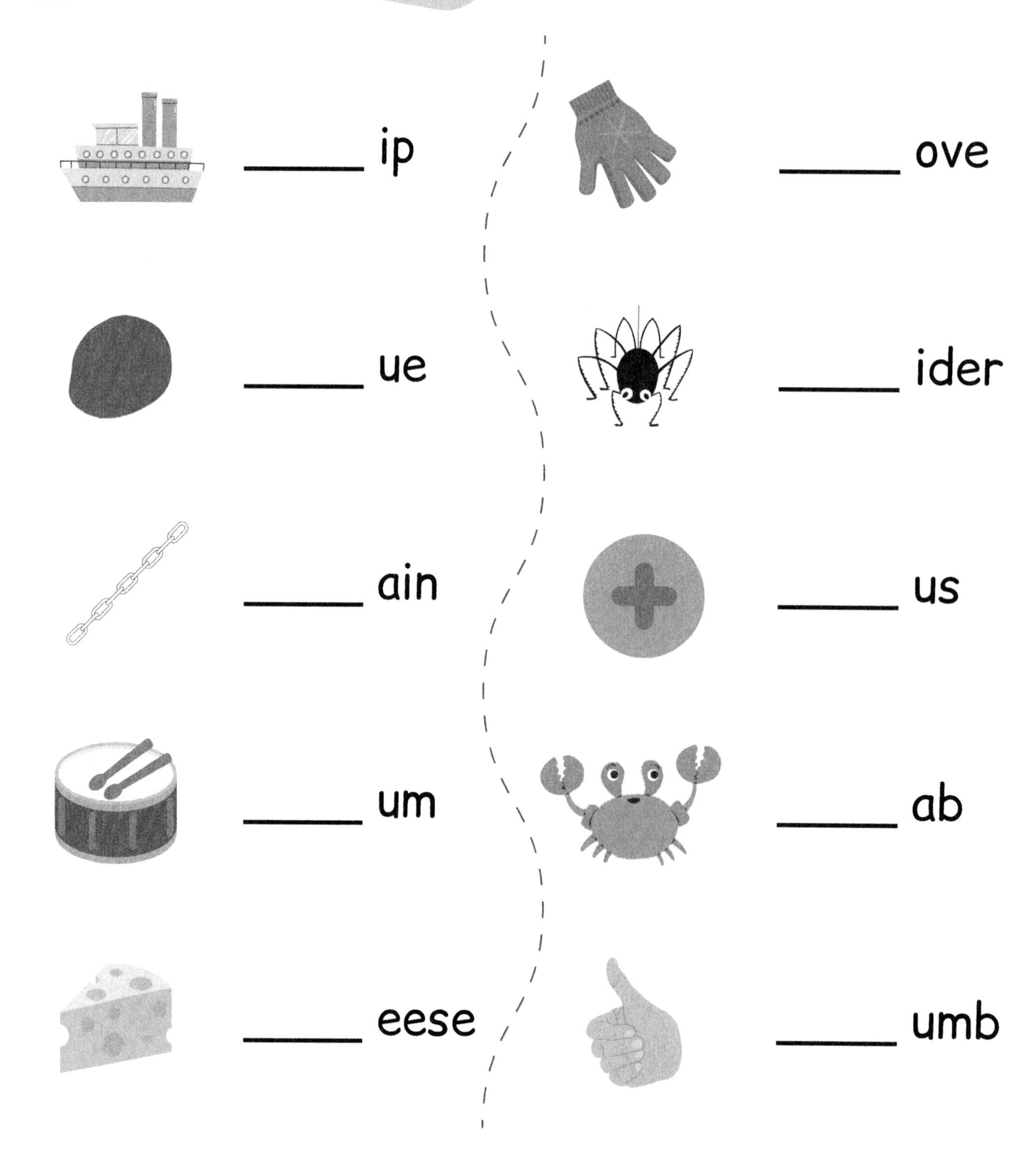

_____ ip

_____ ove

_____ ue

_____ ider

_____ ain

_____ us

_____ um

_____ ab

_____ eese

_____ umb

BLENDING SOUNDS

Draw a line to match the pictures with their blends.

tr

sp

sn

sw

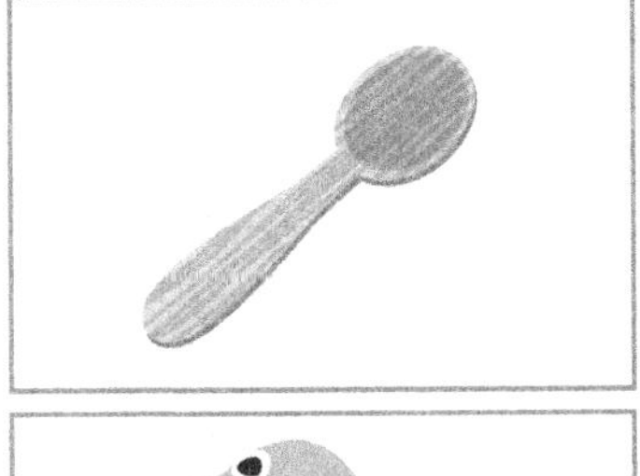

sh

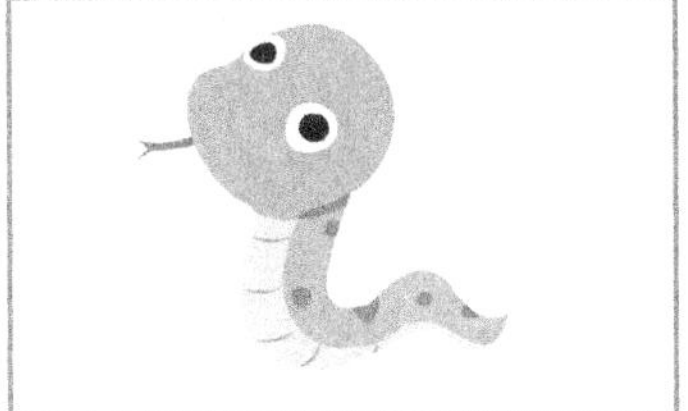

fl

BLENDING SOUNDS

Look at the pictures. Fill in the missing blends to complete the word.

ear ____

____ ock

____ ower

pla ____

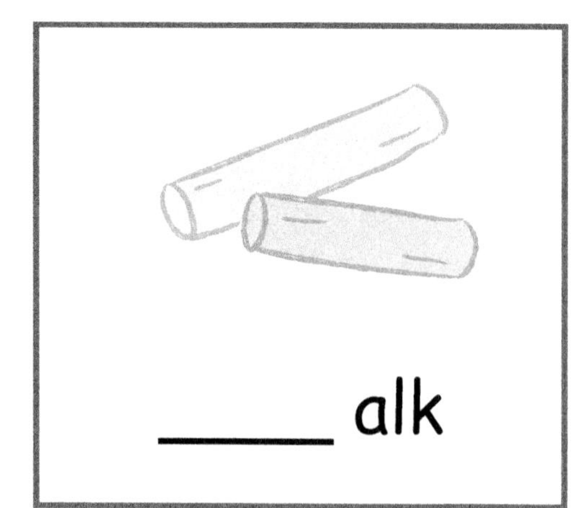

____ alk

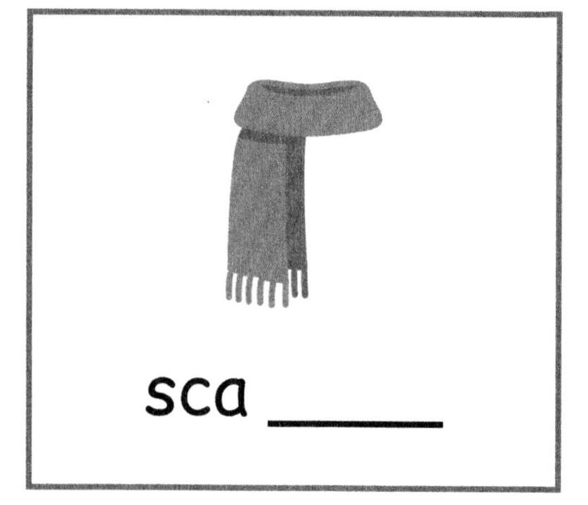

sca ____

BLENDING SOUNDS

Look at the pictures. Write the ending blends for each picture in the box.

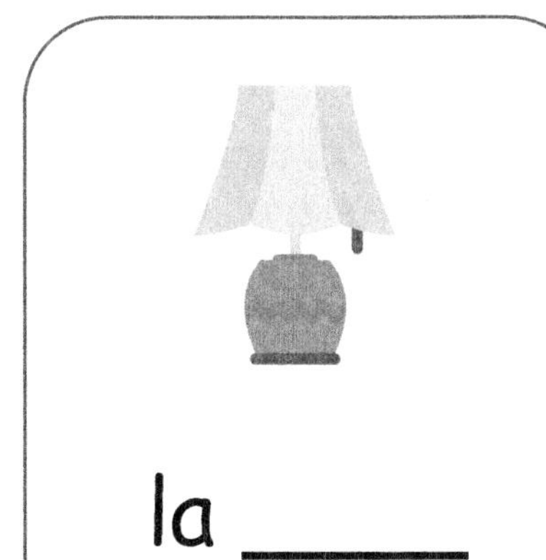

la _____

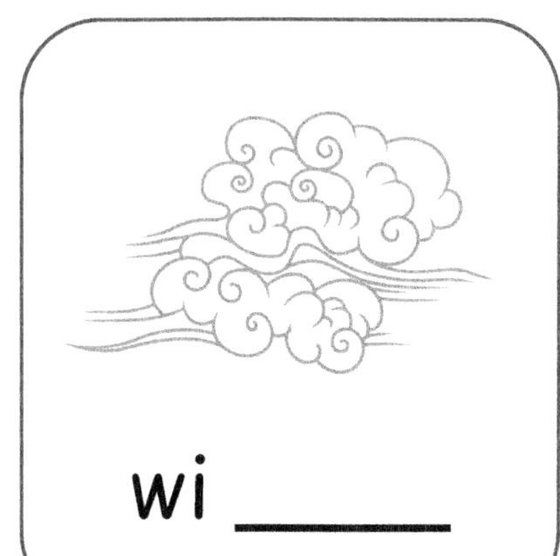

wi _____

ju _____

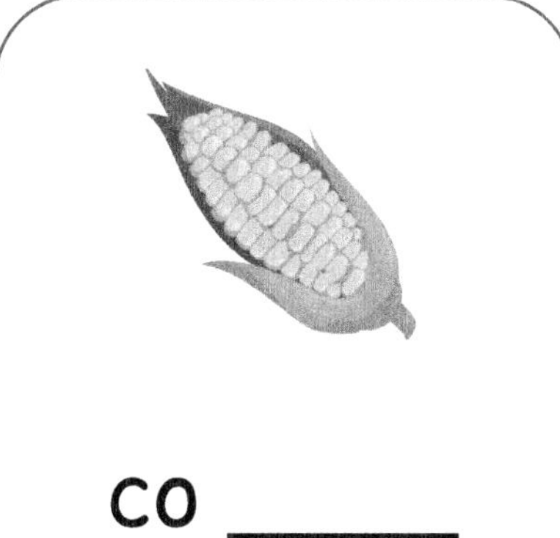

co _____

ne _____

gi _____

ca _____

te _____

de _____

BLENDING SOUNDS

Look at the pictures. Circle the correct ending blend for each picture.

	ck	ik		ik	lk
	fo	og		rt	st
	ra	sa		nd	an
	mb	am		lb	ub
	to	mo		at	nt
	ar	or		nk	mk

SIGHT WORD

"is"

Read and color it.

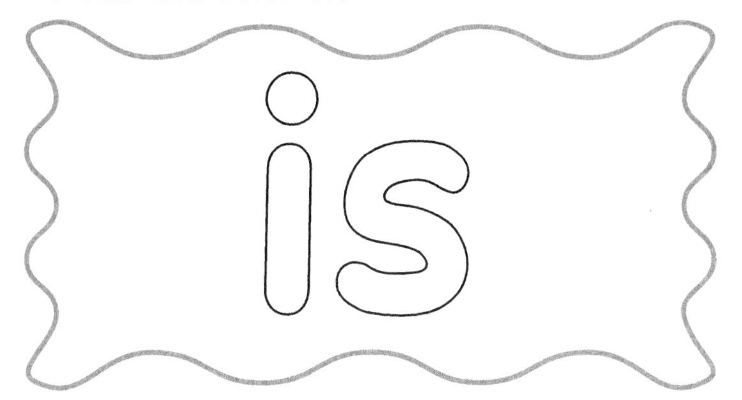

Trace and practice.

is is is is

Find and circle.

am	is	he	is
	it	this	
is	a	is	is

Fill in the missing letter.

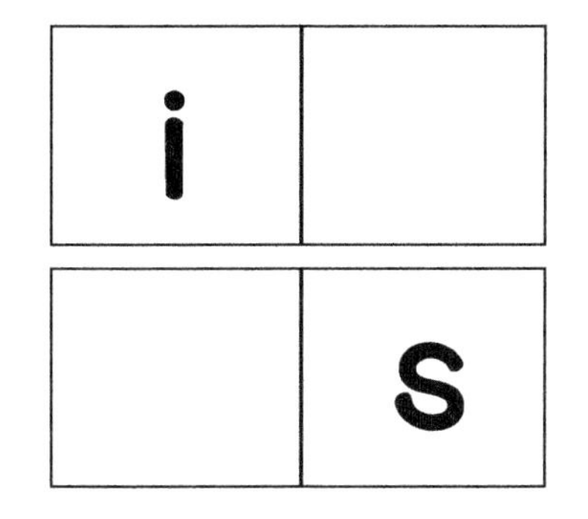

Read and write the word in the sentence.

This ________ a fat cat.

How many syllables?
Color the correct circle.

SIGHT WORD
Read and color it.
an
Trace and practice.
an an an an
Find and circle.
am is he an
an an
is an is it
Fill in the missing letter.
a
n
Read and write the word in the sentence.
It is ice cream.
How many syllables?
Color the correct circle.
1 2 3
68

SIGHT WORD

"am"

Read and color it.

Trace and practice.

am am am am

Find and circle.

am is am this
am on
am up it and

Fill in the missing letter.

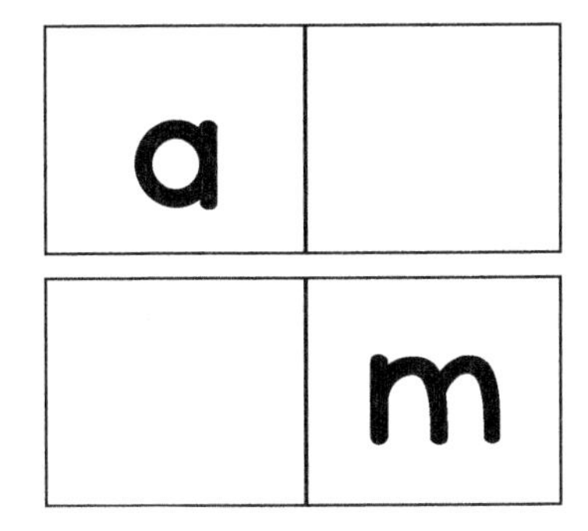

Read and write the word in the sentence.

I ________ drinking water.

How many syllables?
Color the correct circle.

Read and color it.

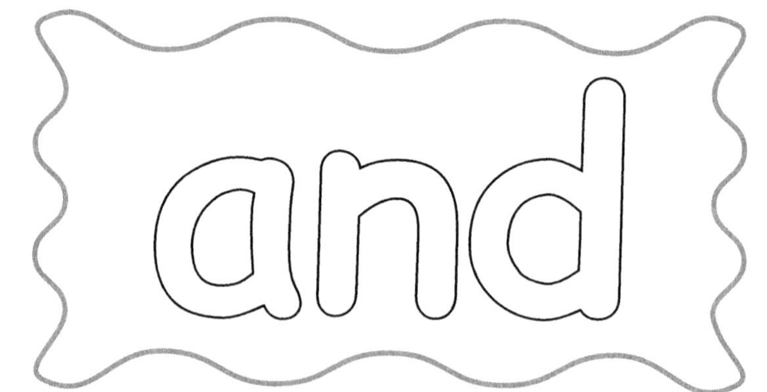

Trace and practice.

and and and and

Find and circle.

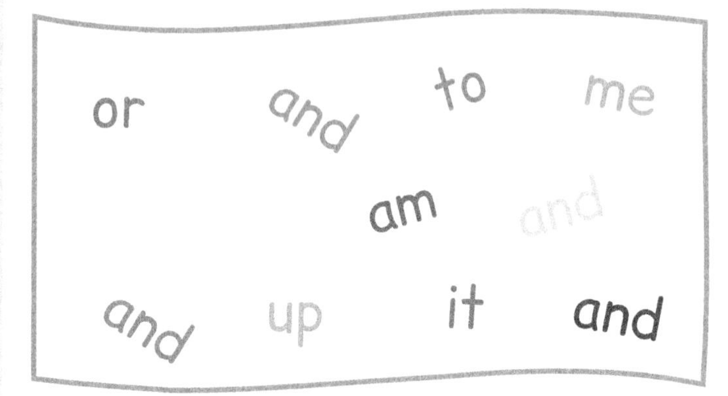

Fill in the missing letter.

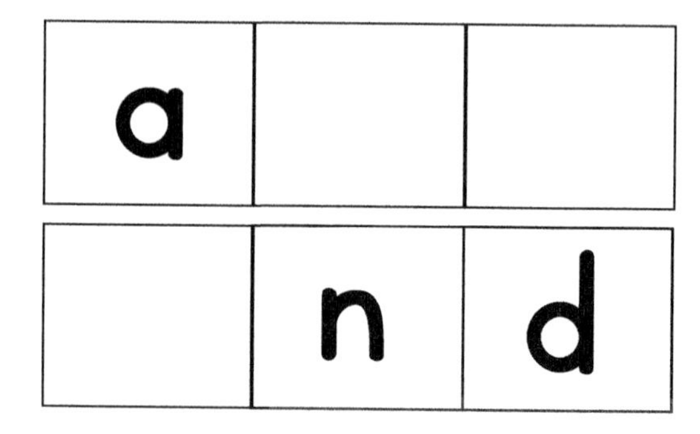

Read and write the word in the sentence.

Nina __________ Jan are playing.

How many syllables?
Color the correct circle.

SIGHT WORD

"can"

Read and color it.

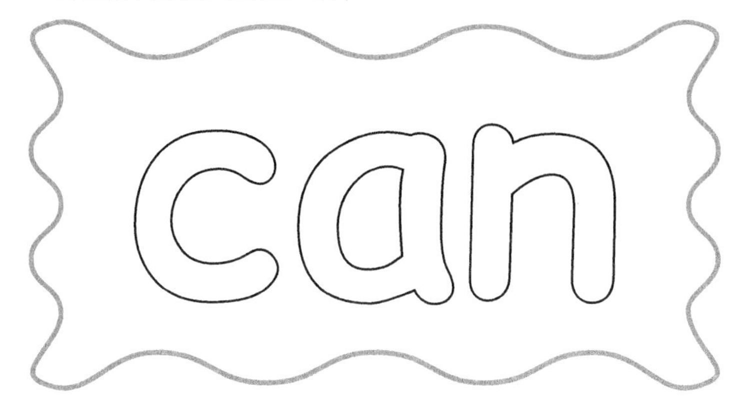

Trace and practice.

can can can can

Find and circle.

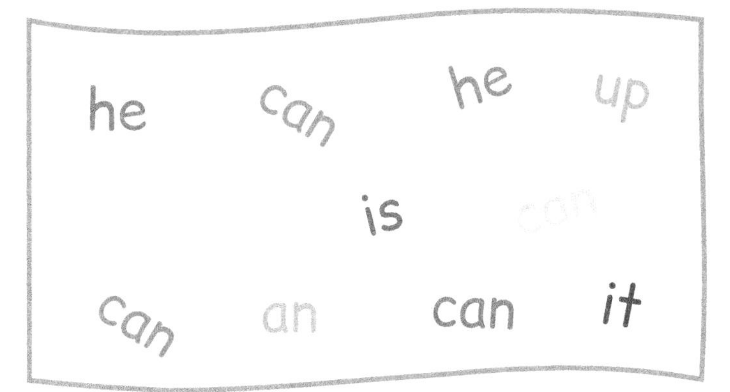

Fill in the missing letter.

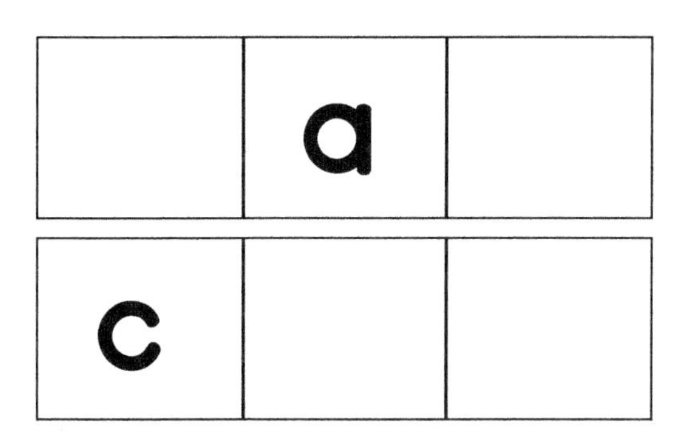

Read and write the word in the sentence.

I ______ sing a song.

How many syllables?
Color the correct circle.

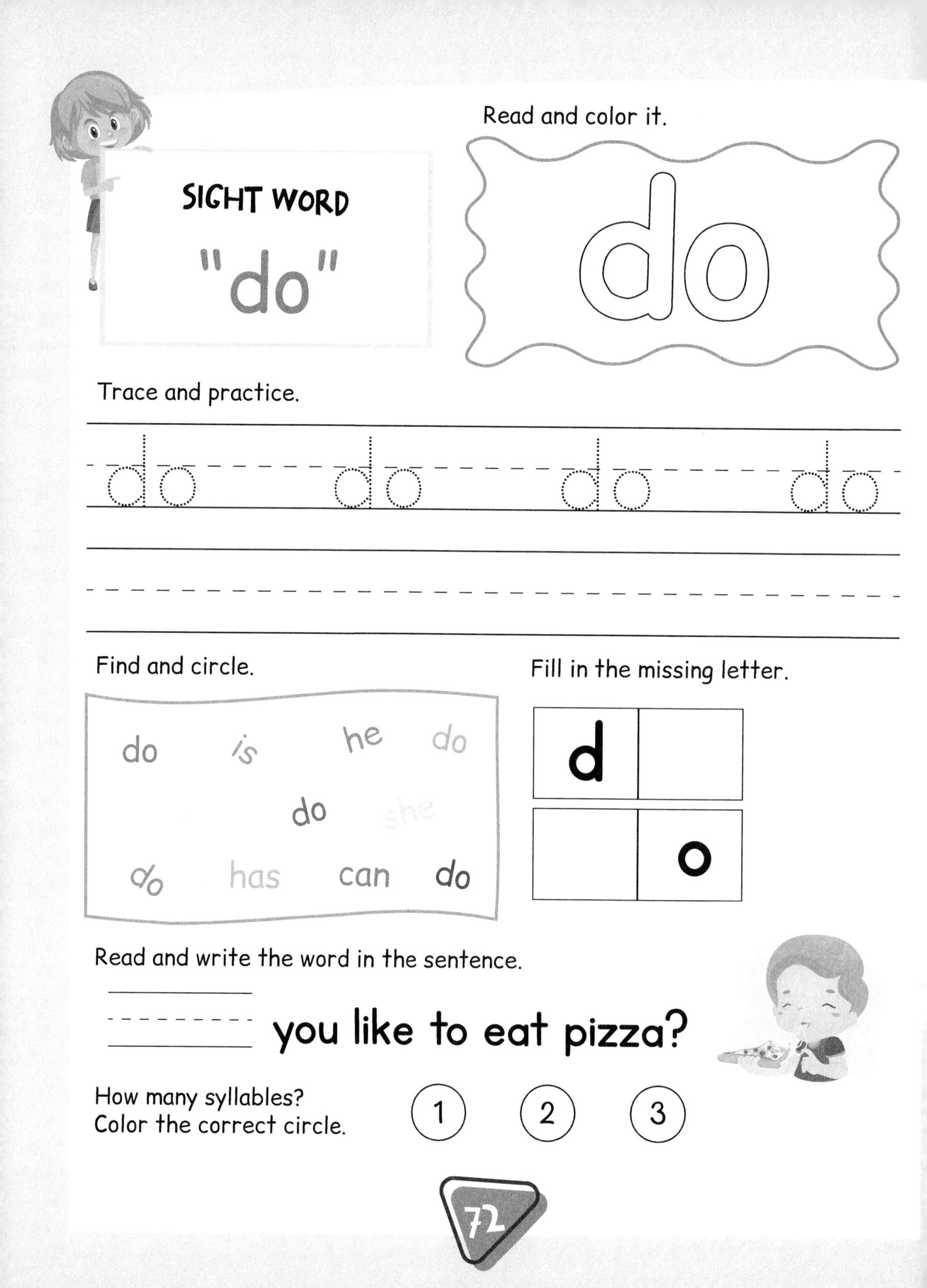
SIGHT WORD
"do"
Read and color it.
do
Trace and practice.
do do do do
Find and circle.
do
is
he
do
do
she
do
has
can
do
Fill in the missing letter.
d
o
Read and write the word in the sentence.
you like to eat pizza?
How many syllables?
Color the correct circle.
1
2
3
72

SIGHT WORD "for"

Read and color it.

Trace and practice.

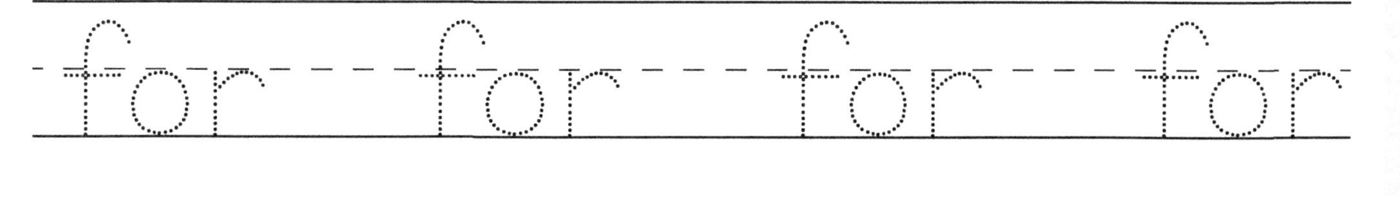

Find and circle.

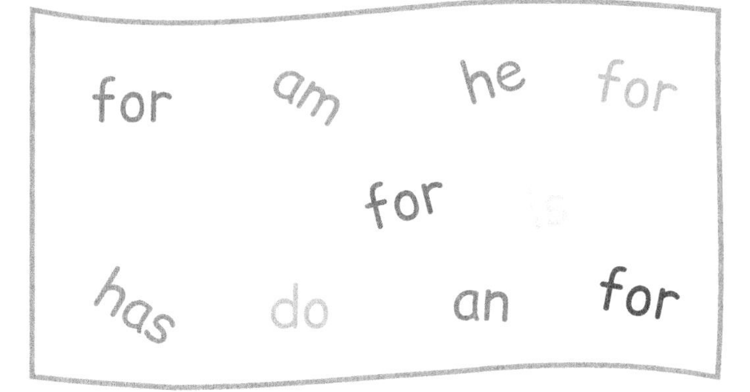

Fill in the missing letter.

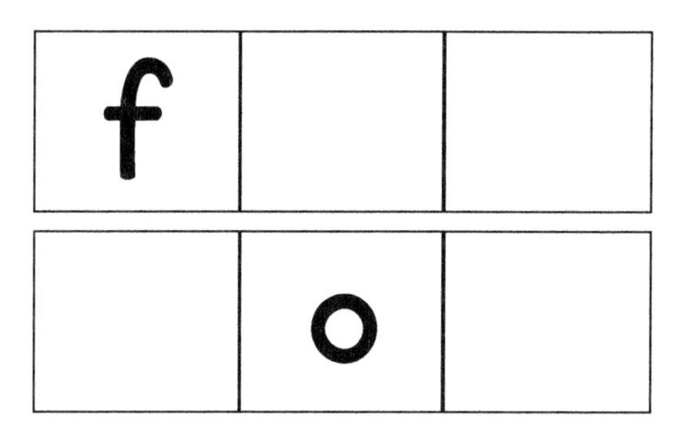

Read and write the word in the sentence.

Go ________ a bath.

How many syllables?
Color the correct circle.

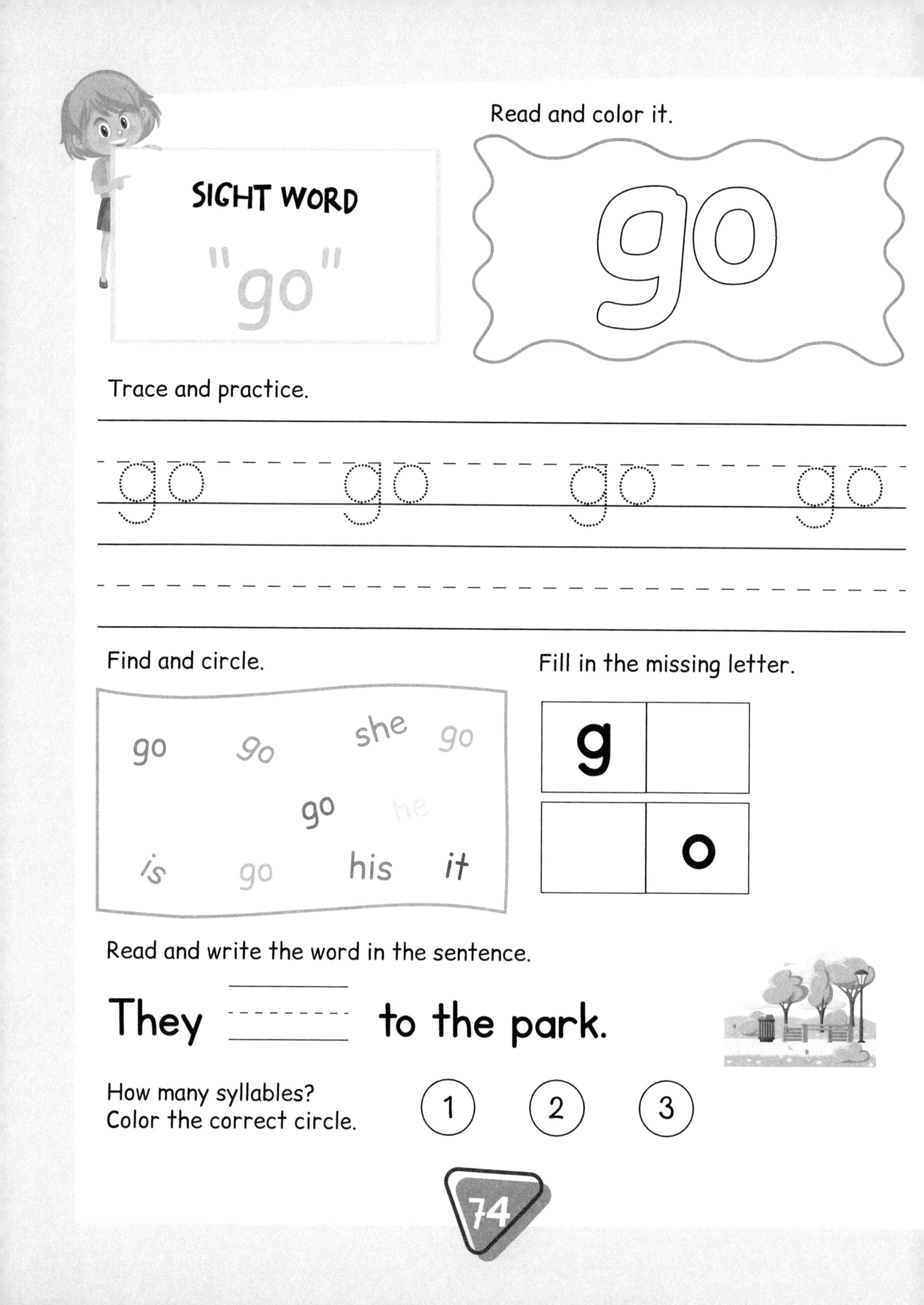
SIGHT WORD
"go"
Read and color it.
go
Trace and practice.
go go go go
Find and circle.
go
go
she
go
go
he
is
go
his
it
Fill in the missing letter.
g
o
Read and write the word in the sentence.
They to the park.
How many syllables?
Color the correct circle.
1
2
3
74

SIGHT WORD

"has"

Read and color it.

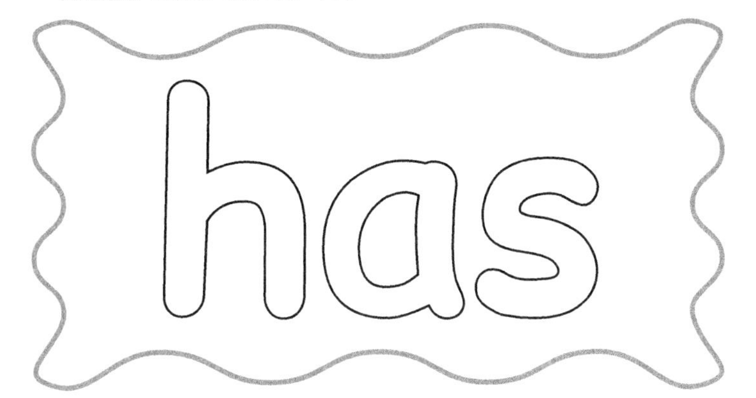

Trace and practice.

has has has has

Find and circle.

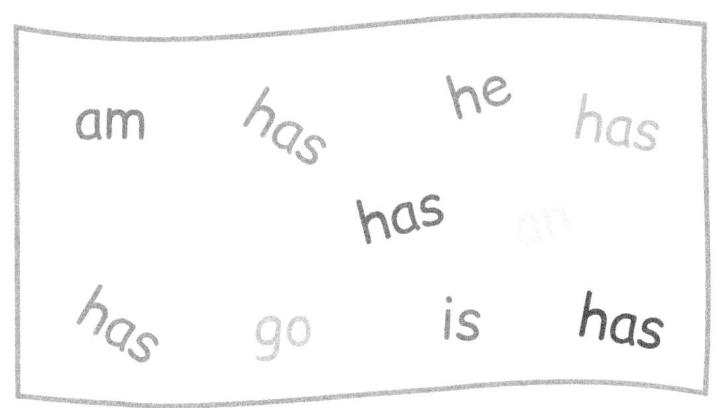

Fill in the missing letter.

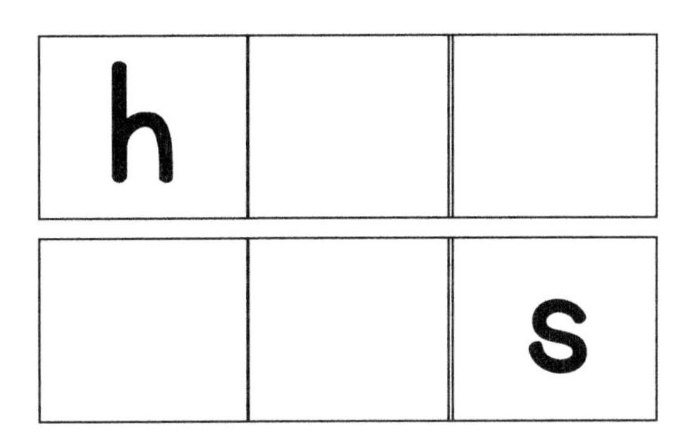

Read and write the word in the sentence.

She ________ a pet.

How many syllables?
Color the correct circle.

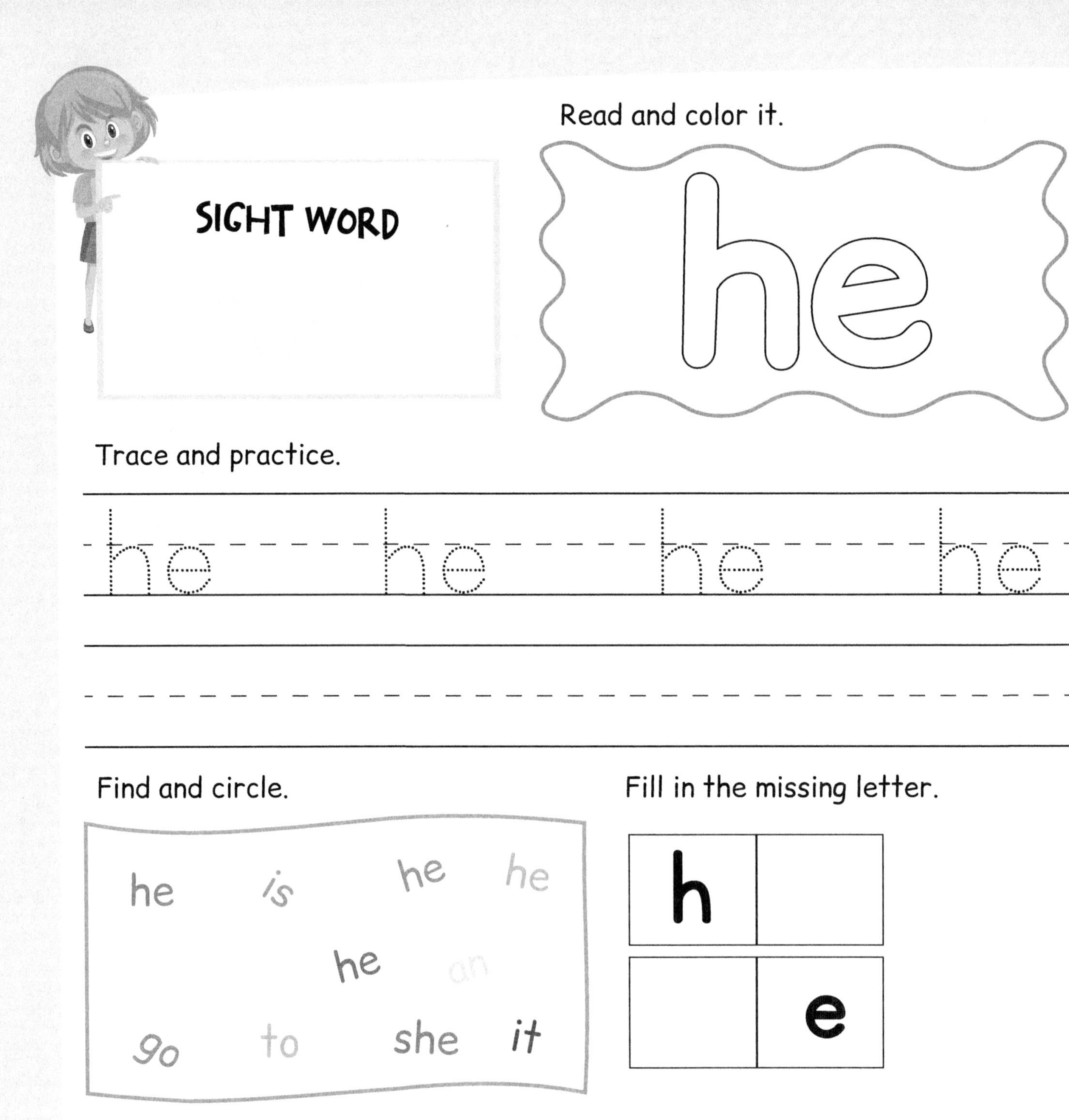

SIGHT WORD

Read and color it.

he

Trace and practice.

he he he he

Find and circle.

he is he he he an go to she it

Fill in the missing letter.

h	
	e

Read and write the word in the sentence.

______ is sleeping.

How many syllables?
Color the correct circle.

1

2

3

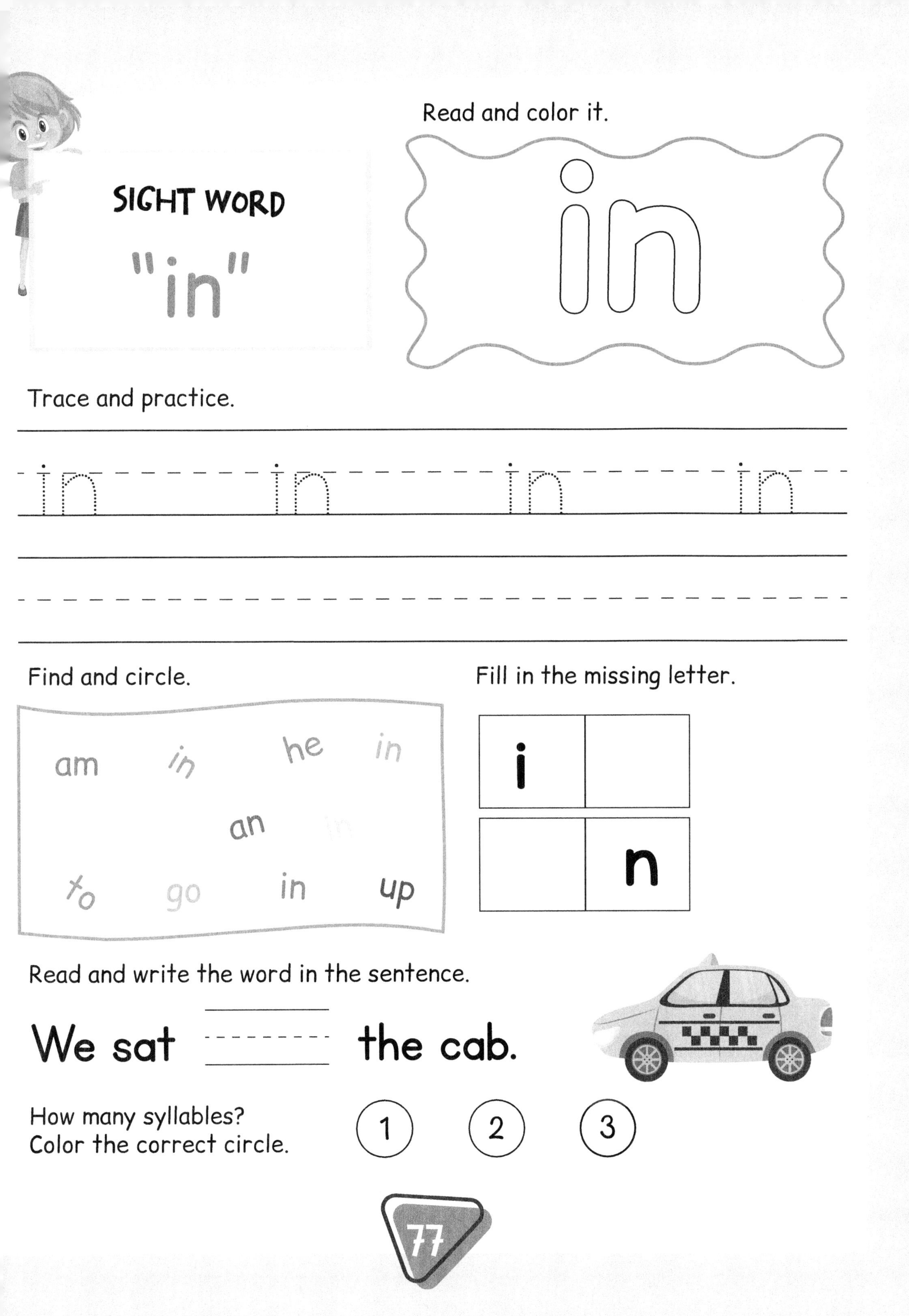
SIGHT WORD
"in"
Read and color it.
in
Trace and practice.
in in in in
Find and circle.
am in he in
an in
to go in up
Fill in the missing letter.
i
n
Read and write the word in the sentence.
We sat the cab.
How many syllables?
Color the correct circle.
1 2 3

Read and color it.

Trace and practice.

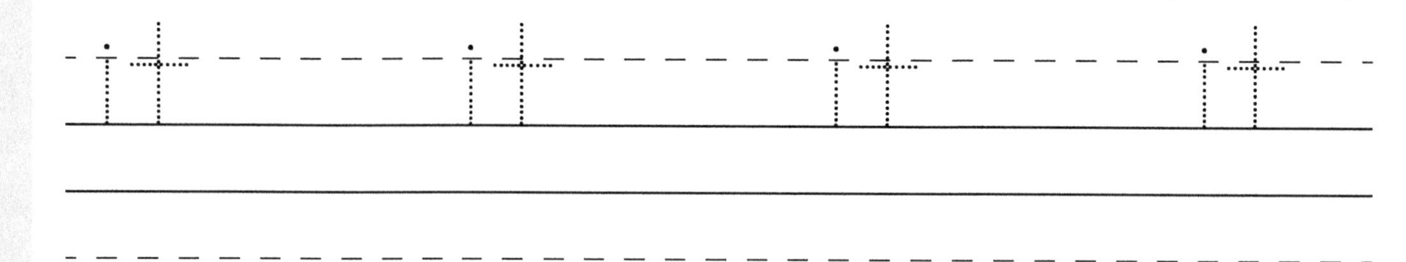

Find and circle.

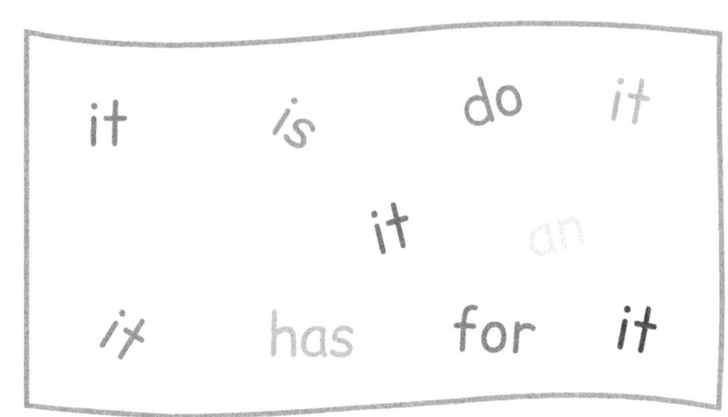

Fill in the missing letter.

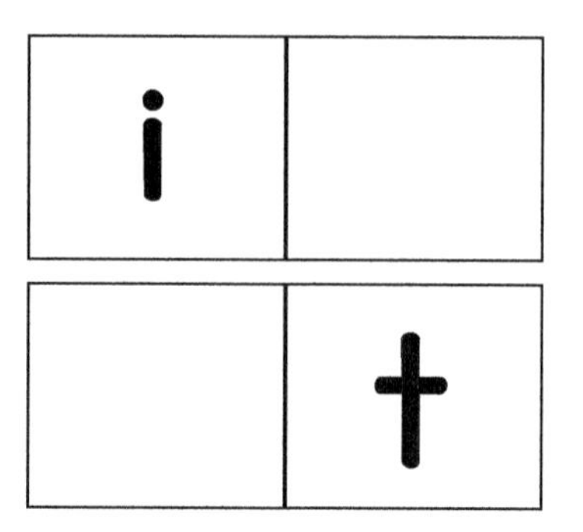

Read and write the word in the sentence.

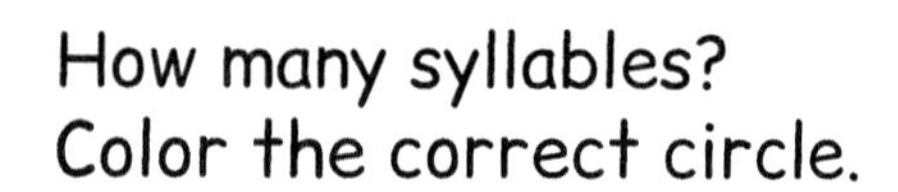 **is raining.**

How many syllables?
Color the correct circle.

SIGHT WORD

"but"

Read and color it.

Trace and practice.

but but but but

Find and circle.

he but he up
is but
but an but it

Fill in the missing letter.

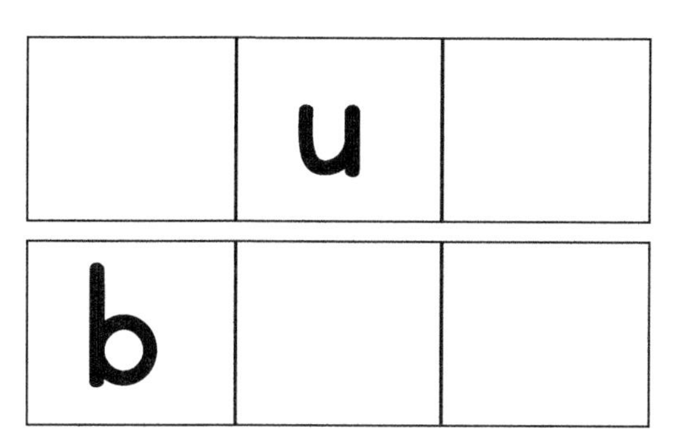

Read and write the word in the sentence.

There was no one at the library ________ me.

How many syllables?
Color the correct circle.

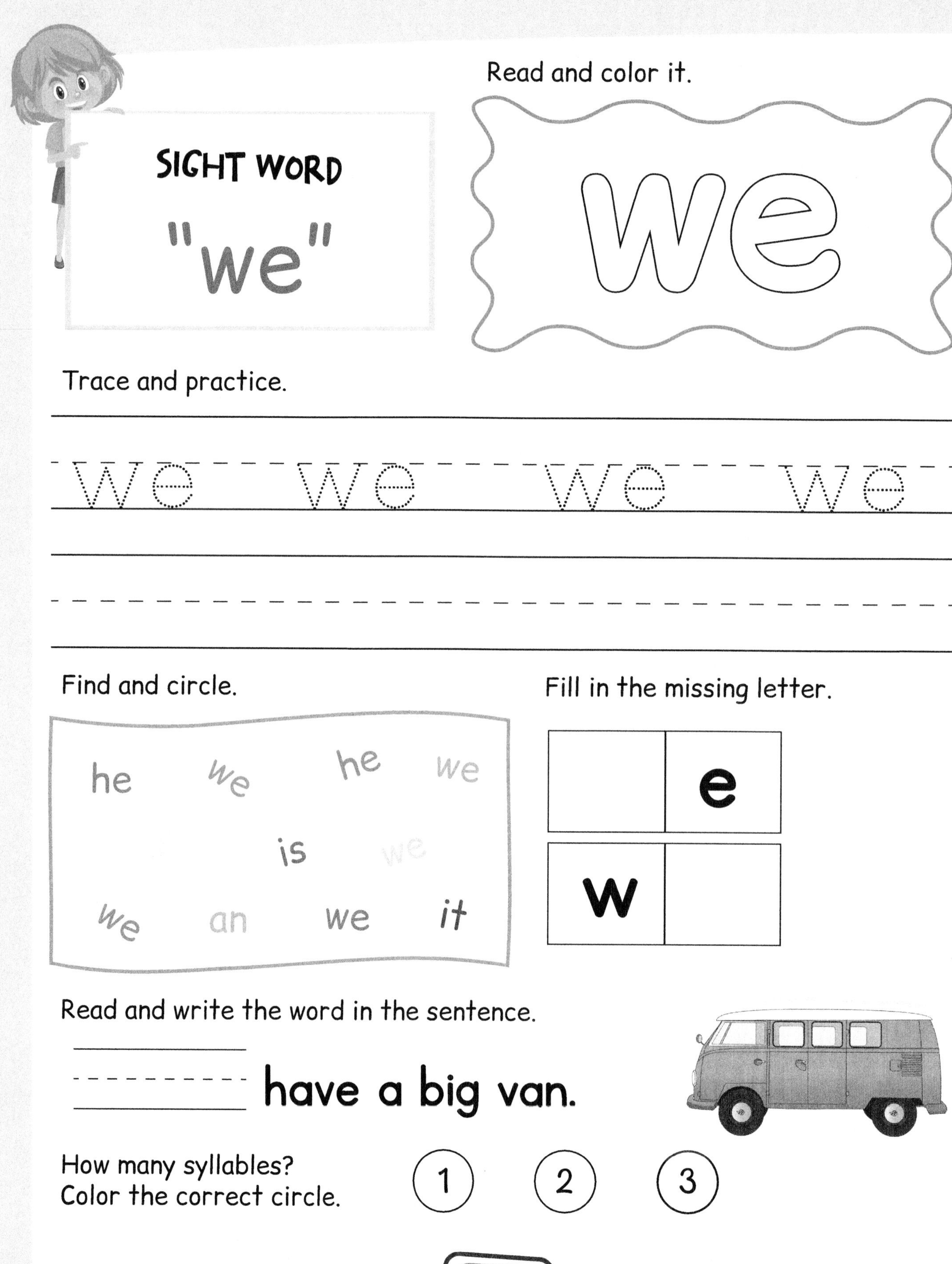
SIGHT WORD
"we"
Read and color it.
we
Trace and practice.
we we we we
Find and circle.
he
we
he
we
is
we
we
an
we
it
Fill in the missing letter.
e
w
Read and write the word in the sentence.
have a big van.
How many syllables?
Color the correct circle.
1
2
3

SIGHT WORD

"no"

Read and color it.

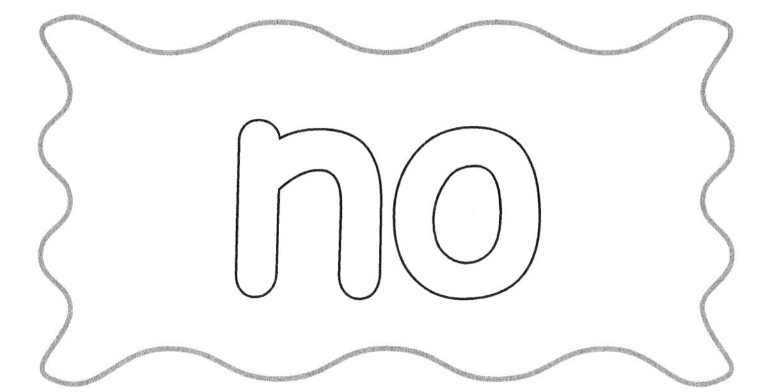

Trace and practice.

no no no no

Find and circle.

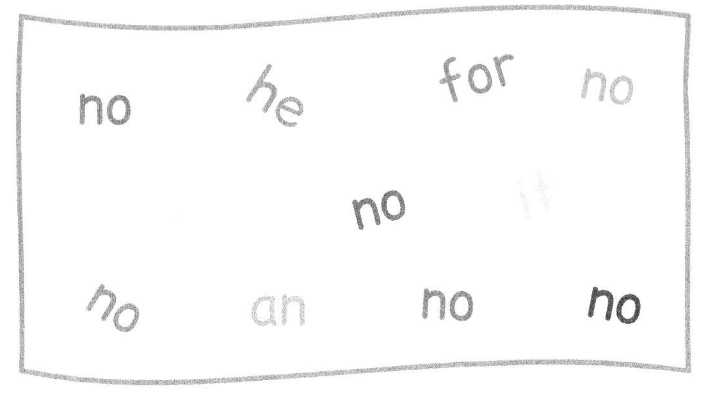

Fill in the missing letter.

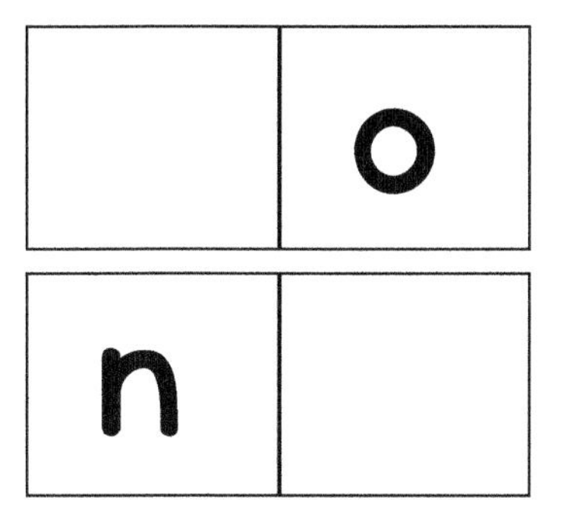

Read and write the word in the sentence.

I have ________ car.

How many syllables?
Color the correct circle.

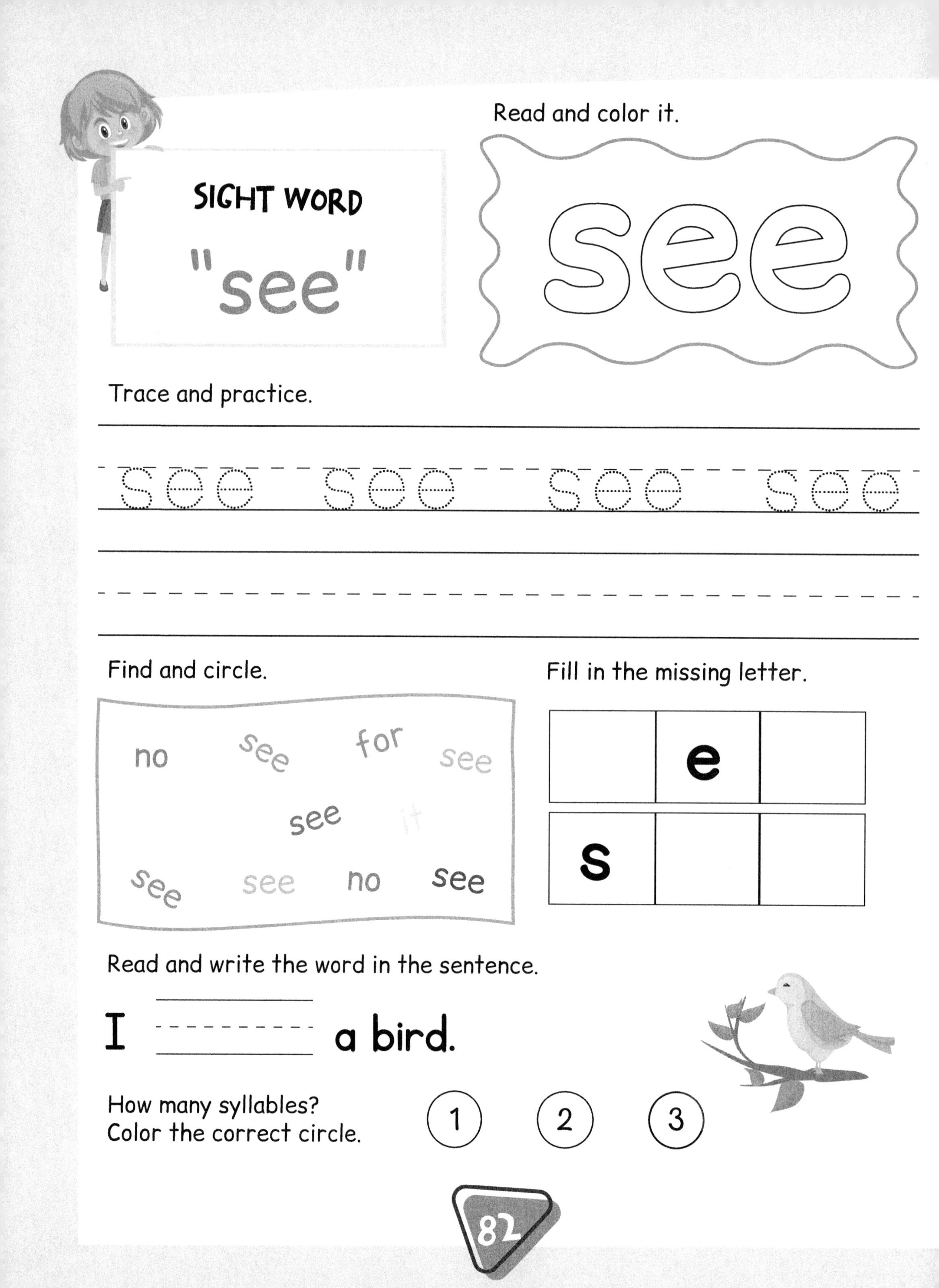
SIGHT WORD
"see"
Read and color it.
see
Trace and practice.
see see see see
Find and circle.
no
see
for
see
see
it
see
see
no
see
Fill in the missing letter.
e
s
Read and write the word in the sentence.
I a bird.
How many syllables?
Color the correct circle.
1
2
3
82

SIGHT WORD

"the"

Read and color it.

Trace and practice.

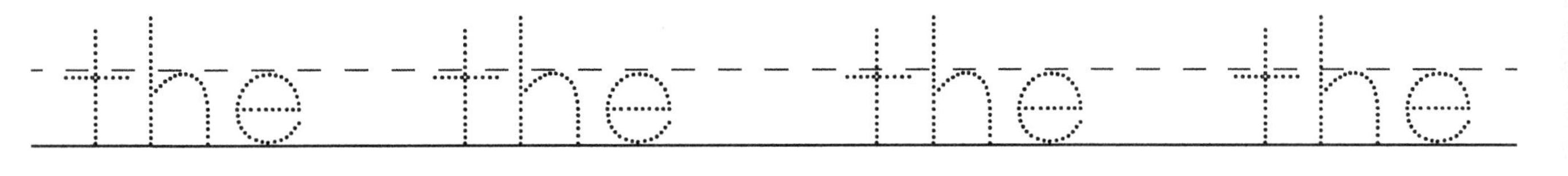

Find and circle.

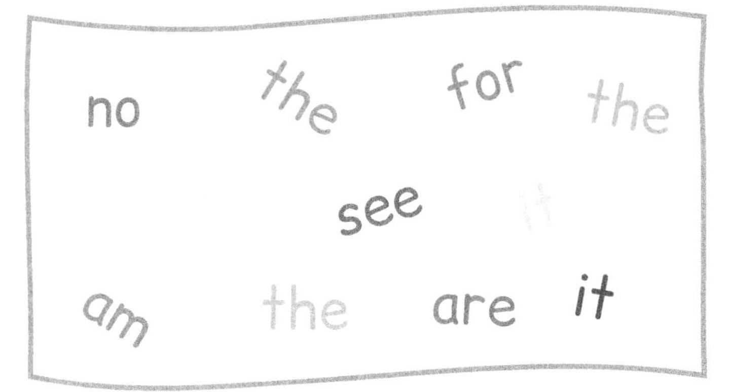

Fill in the missing letter.

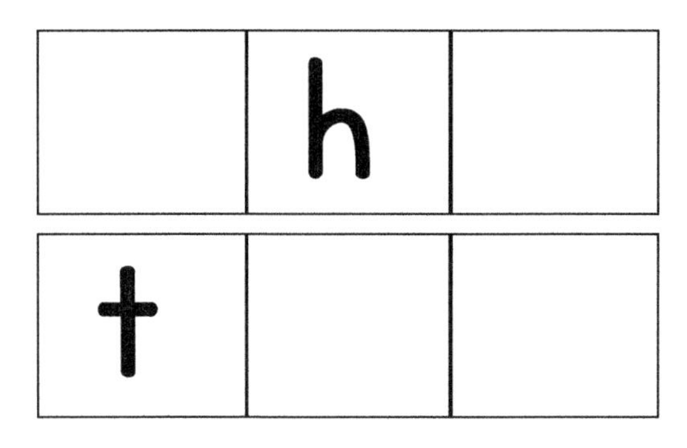

Read and write the word in the sentence.

Look at ________ green frog.

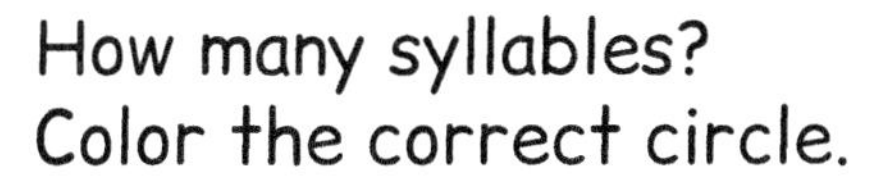
How many syllables?
Color the correct circle.

Read and color it.

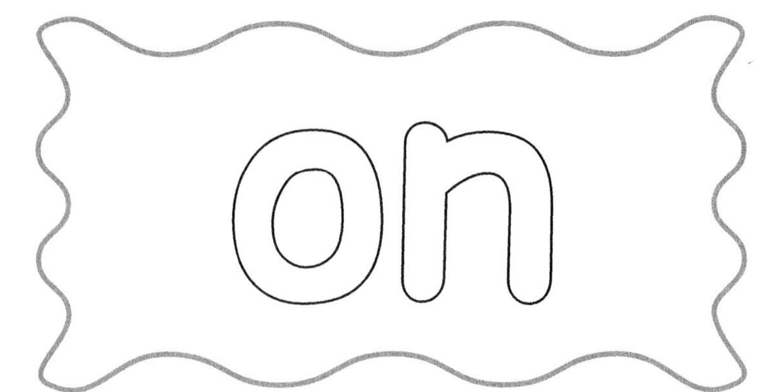

Trace and practice.

on on on on

Find and circle.

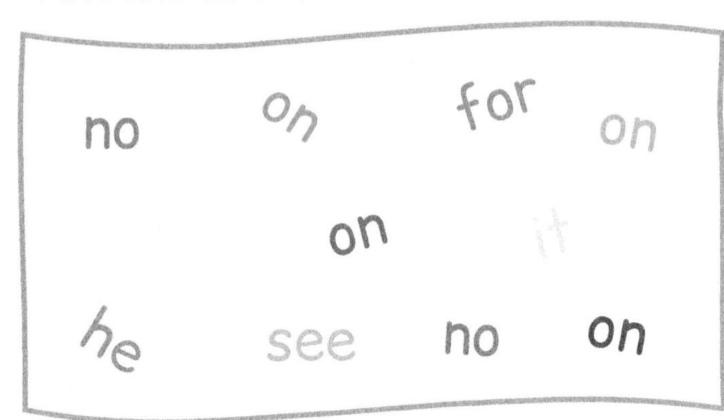

Fill in the missing letter.

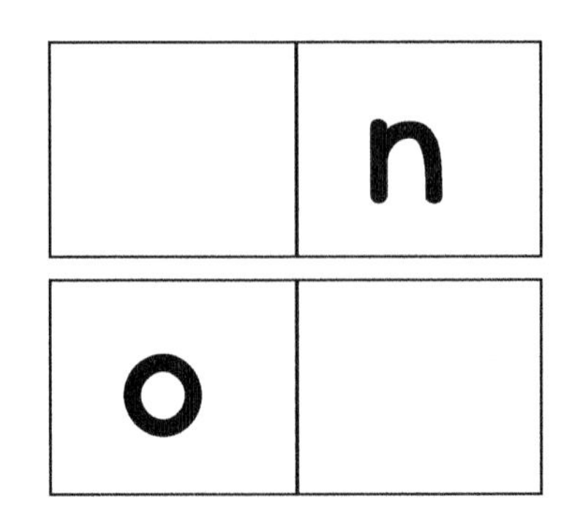

Read and write the word in the sentence.

We sat ______ the mat.

How many syllables?
Color the correct circle.

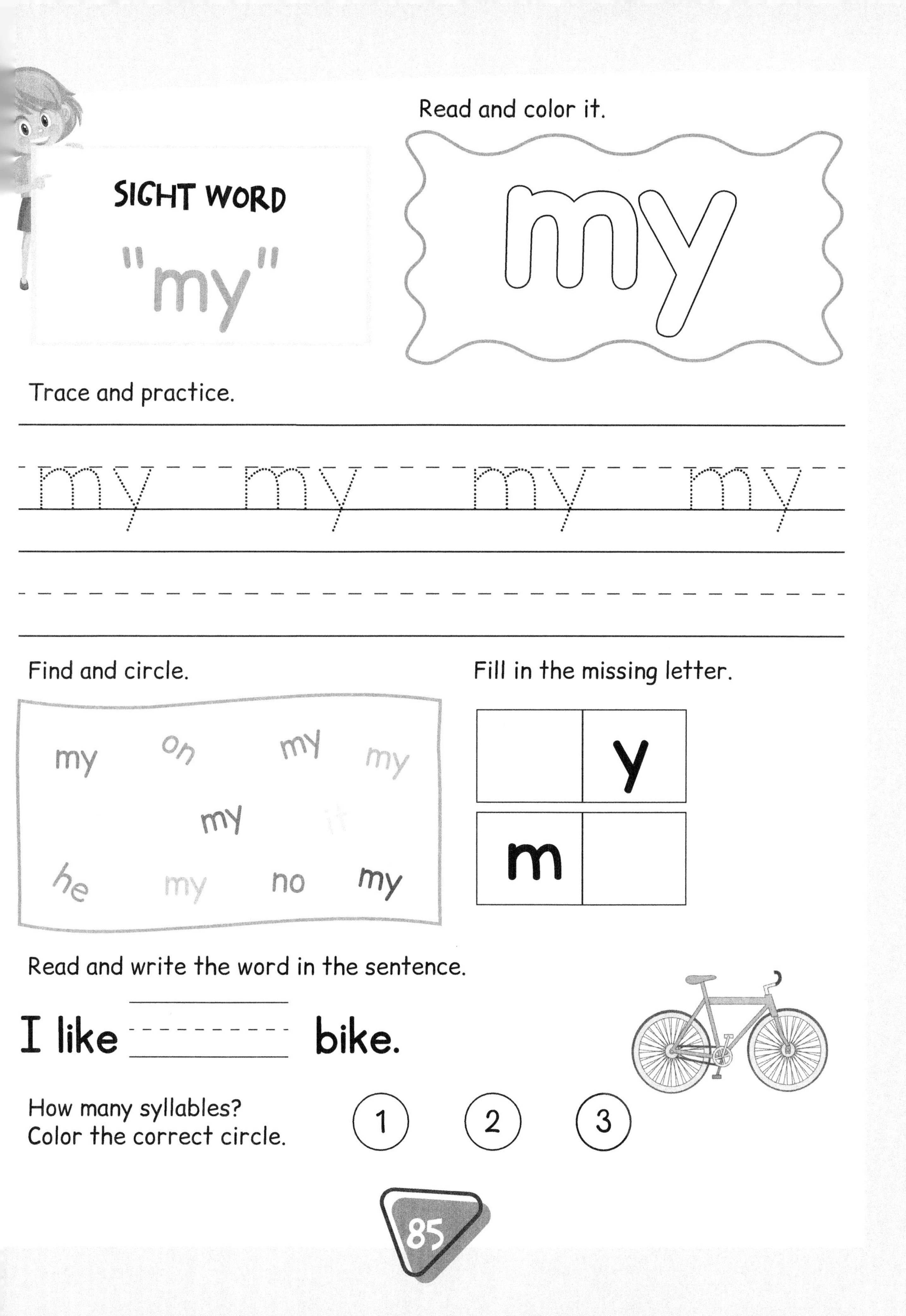
SIGHT WORD
"my"
Read and color it.
my
Trace and practice.
my my my my
Find and circle.
my on my my
my it
he my no my
Fill in the missing letter.
y
m
Read and write the word in the sentence.
I like ________ bike.
How many syllables?
Color the correct circle.
1 2 3

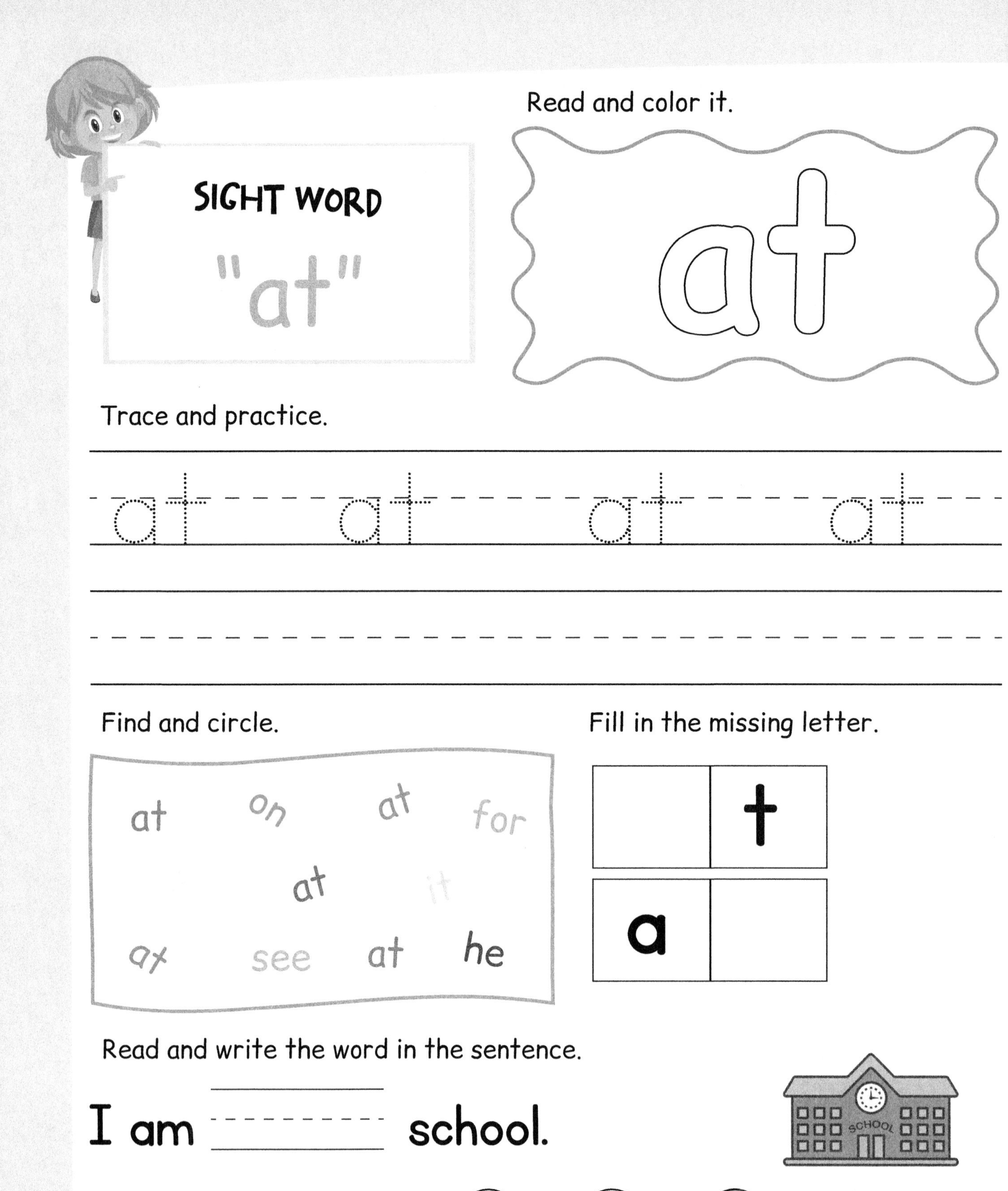

SIGHT WORD

"at"

Read and color it.

at

Trace and practice.

at at at at

Find and circle.

at on at for
at it
at see at he

Fill in the missing letter.

	t
a	

Read and write the word in the sentence.

I am ________ school.

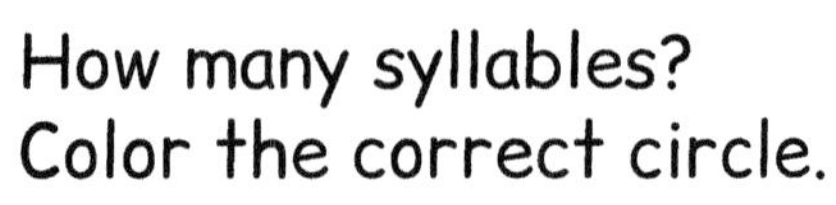

How many syllables?
Color the correct circle.

1

2

3

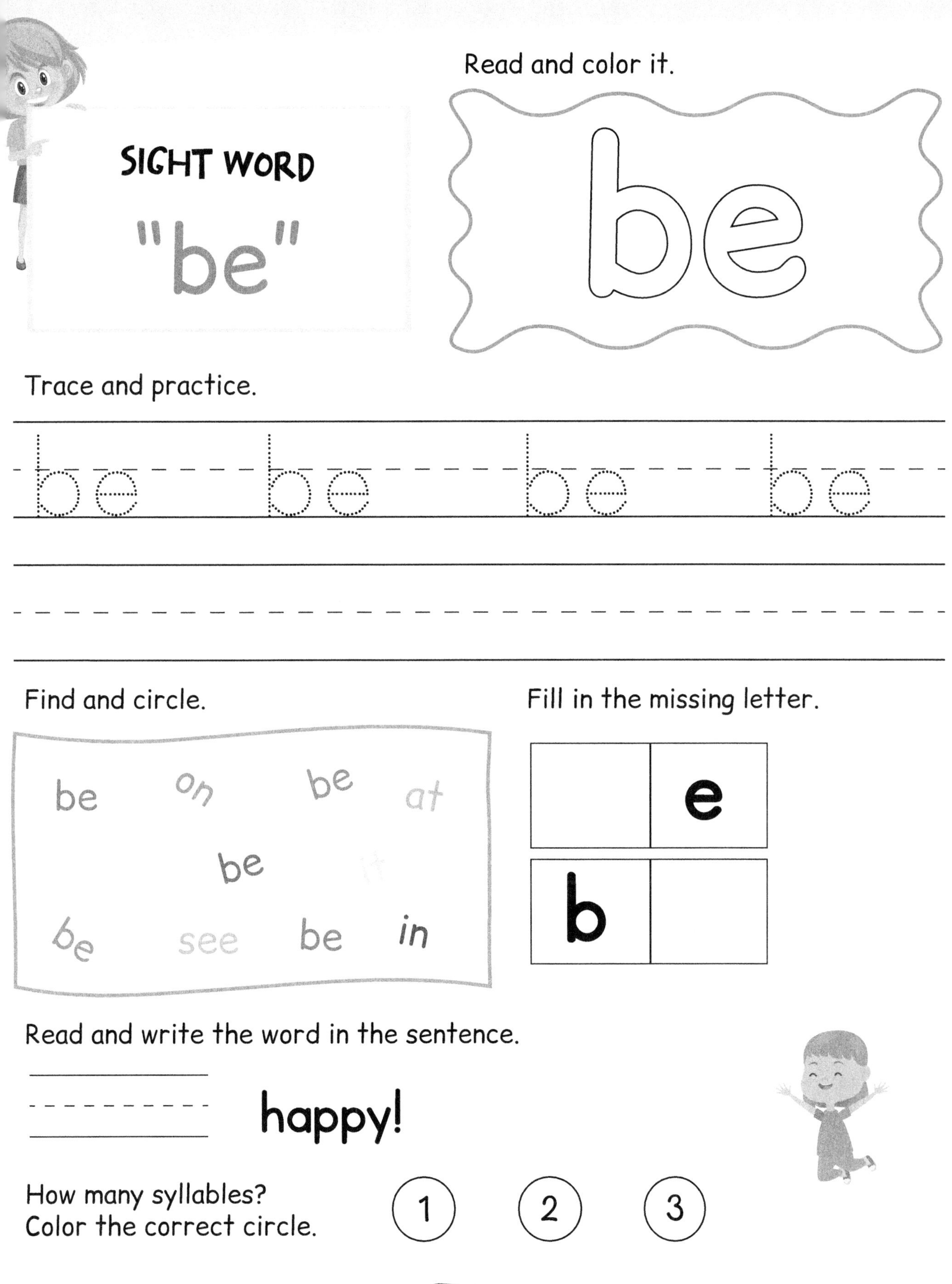

How many syllables?
Color the correct circle.

1 2 3

SIGHT WORD

"are"

Read and color it.

Trace and practice.

are are are are

Find and circle.

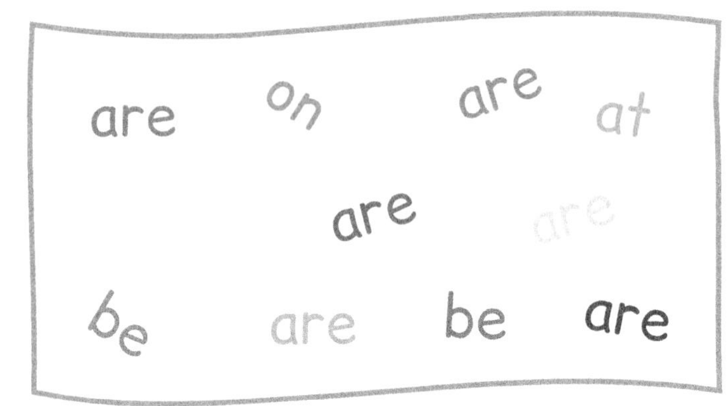

Fill in the missing letter.

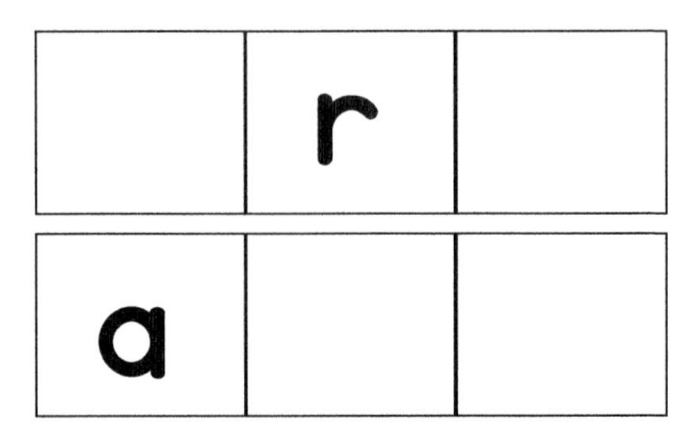

Read and write the word in the sentence.

They 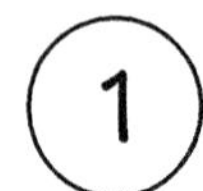 playing.

How many syllables?
Color the correct circle.

  1 2 3

SIGHT WORD

"you"

Read and color it.

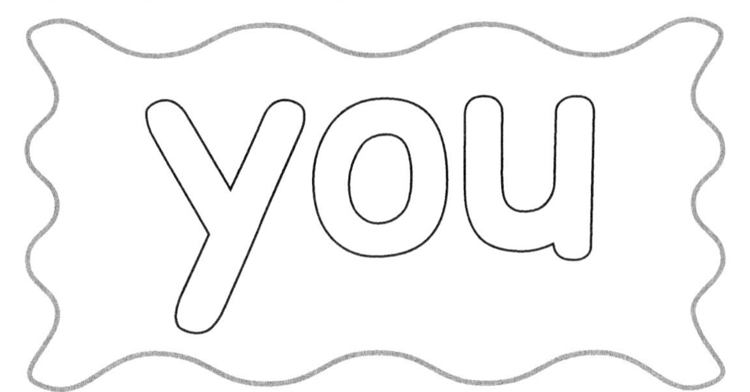

Trace and practice.

you you you you

Find and circle.

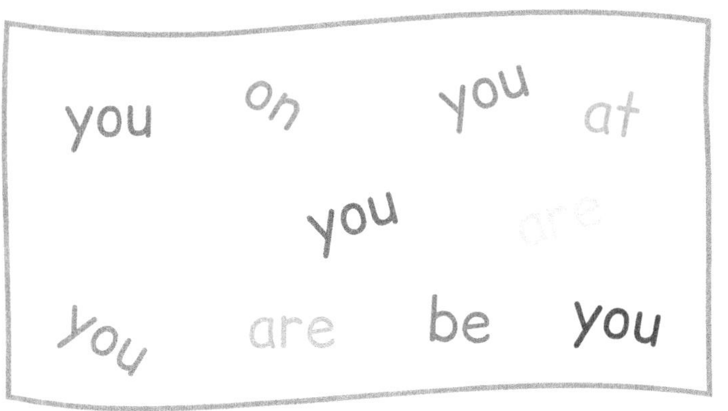

Fill in the missing letter.

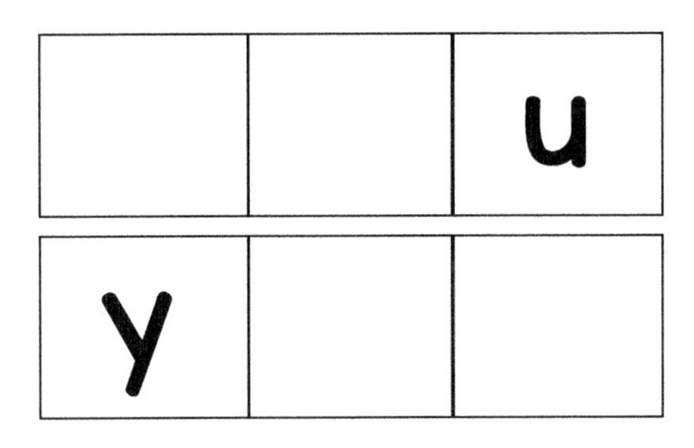

Read and write the word in the sentence.

See __________ tomorrow.

How many syllables?
Color the correct circle.

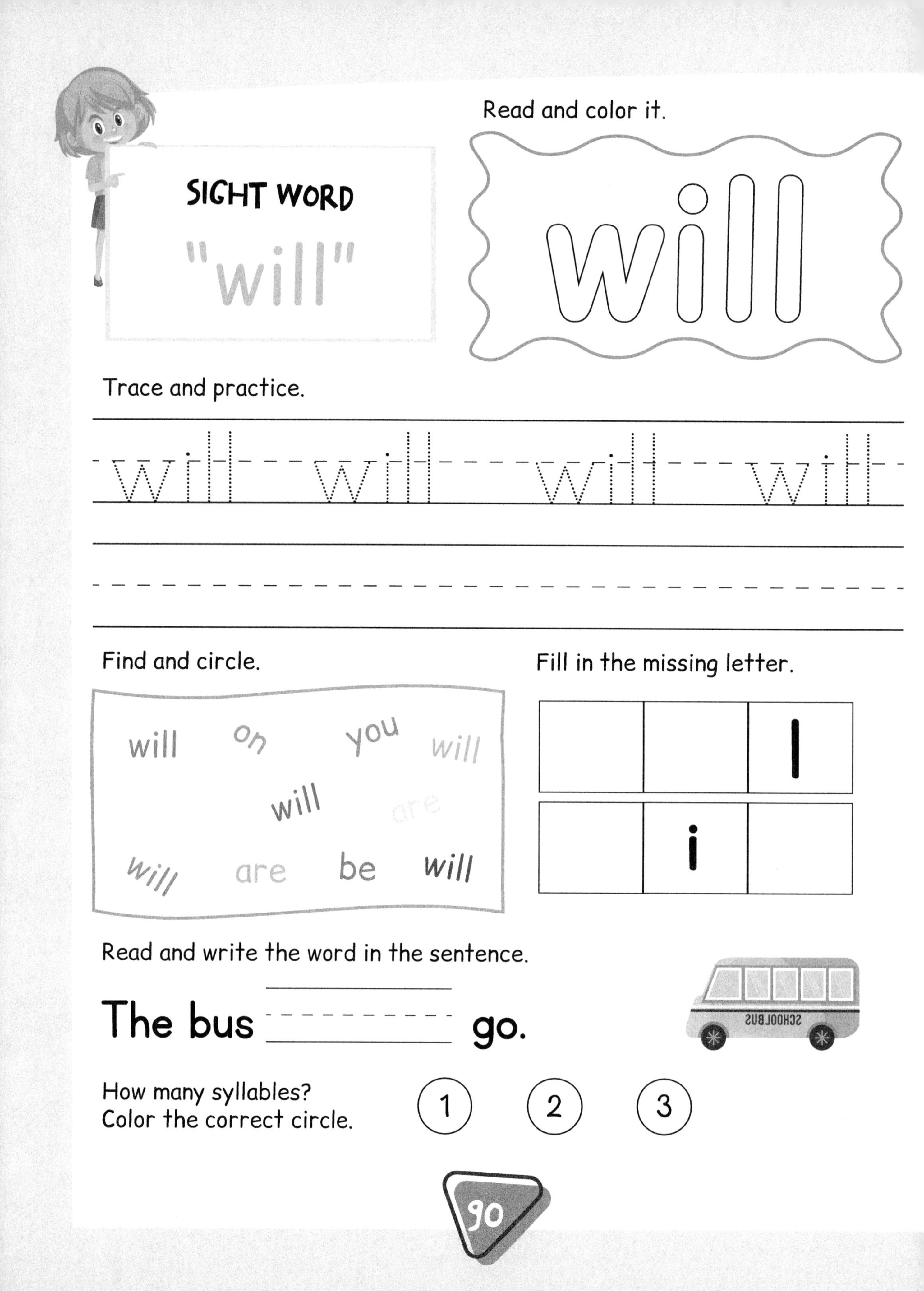
SIGHT WORD
"will"
Read and color it.
will
Trace and practice.
will will will will
Find and circle.
will on you will
will are
will are be will
Fill in the missing letter.
l
i
Read and write the word in the sentence.
The bus ________ go.
SCHOOL BUS
How many syllables?
Color the correct circle.
1 2 3
90

HOMOPHONES

Shade the word that names each picture.

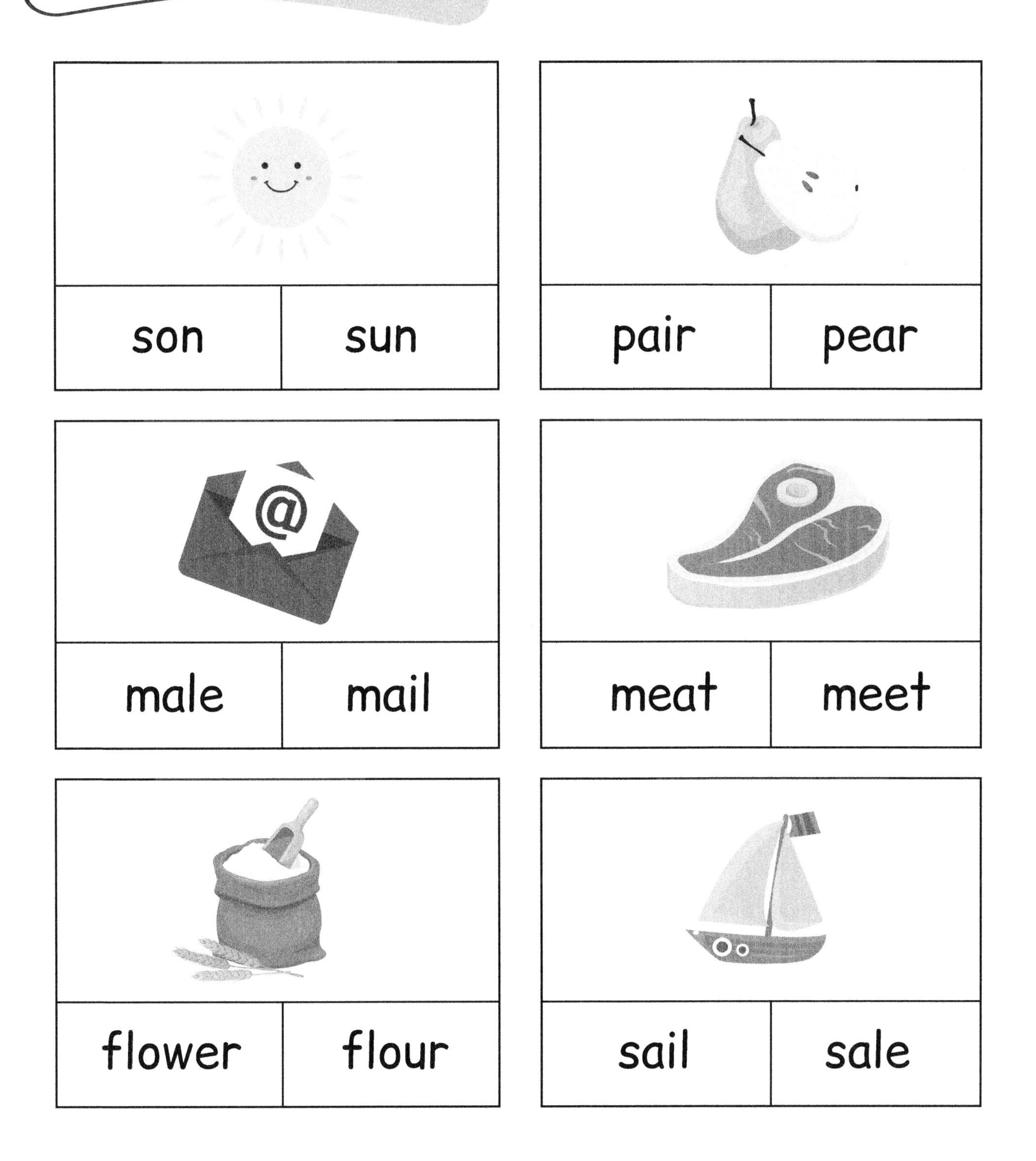

HOMOPHONES

Say the name of each picture out loud. Draw a line between the pictures that sound the same.

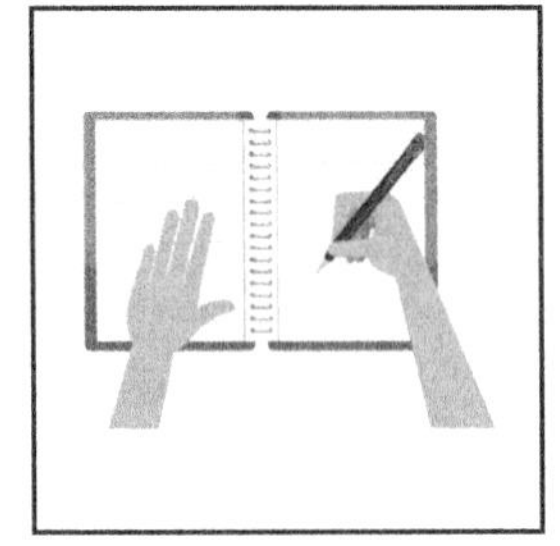

HOMOPHONES

Read the sentence. Choose the correct homophone for each sentence below.

I [ ] in my notebook. (right/write)

Do you [ ] ? (know/no)

I have [ ] pencil. (one/won)

Do not [ ] sad. (bee/be)

This car is brand [ ] . (new/knew)

I did not get [ ] . (male/mail)

Jimmy [ ] a horse. (road/rode)

HOMOPHONES

Read the words. Write the homophones for each word.

sea		sail	
by		grate	
wood		wail	
to		waist	
blew		flu	
boar		witch	
pale		fair	

HOMOPHONES

Say the name of each picture out loud. Write the word that sounds the same as the name of the picture.

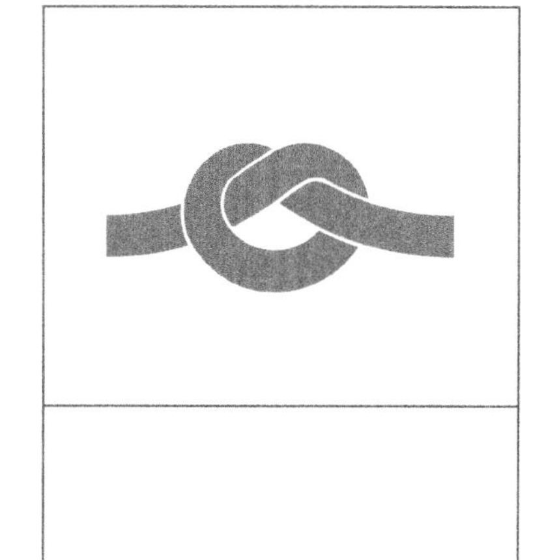

CVC WORDS

Look at the picture in each box. Say the name. Write the word.

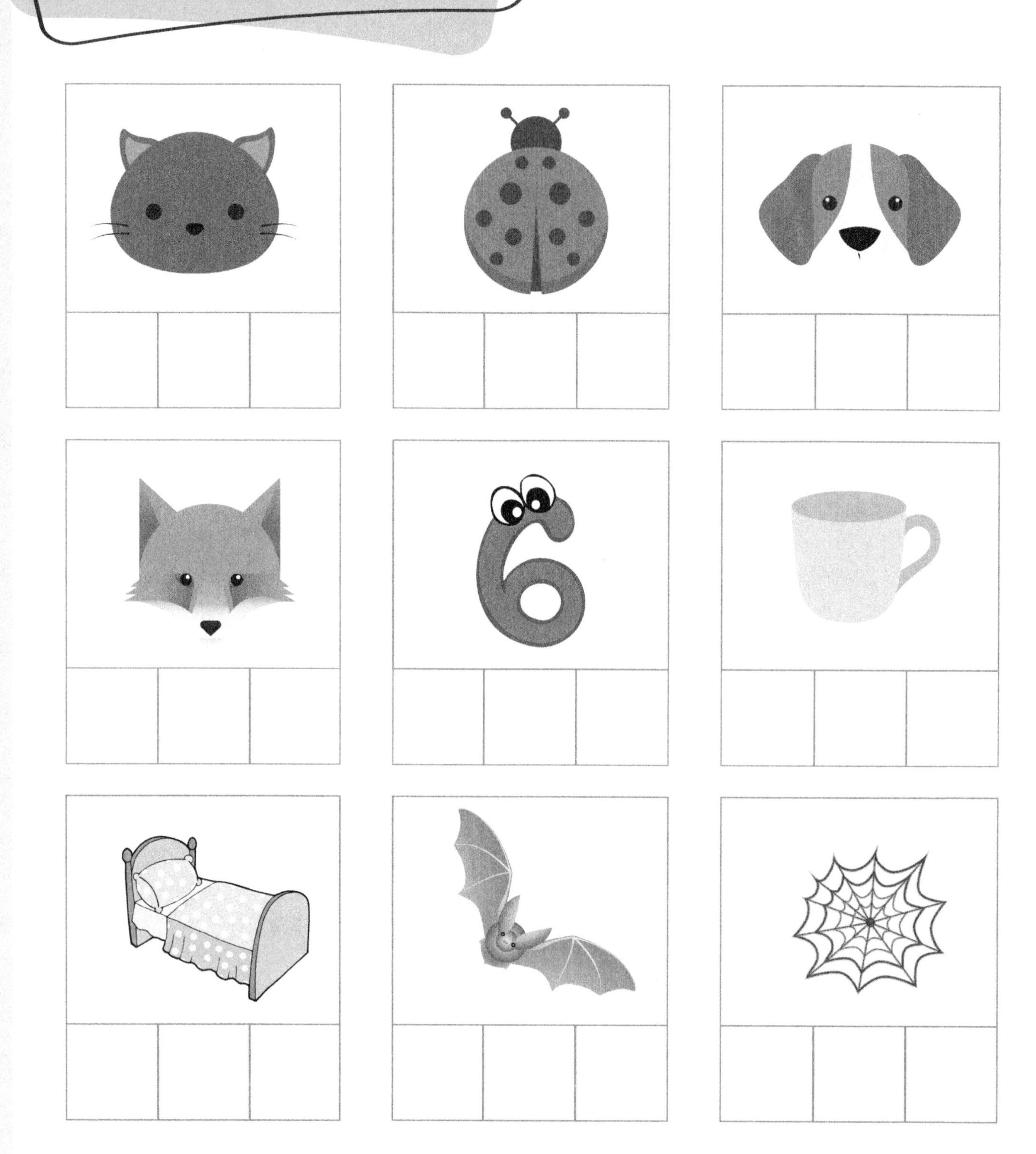

CVC WORDS

Write the missing letter for each word to complete the cvc word.

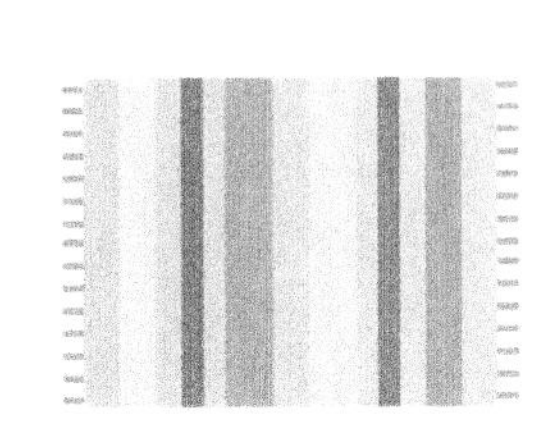 r___ g	 ___ at	 fa ___
 j ___ t	 pe ___	 ___ at
 b ___ x	 ba ___	 p ___ g

CVC WORDS

Look at the pictures. Unscramble the letters to make a word that matches each picture. Write the word in the space.

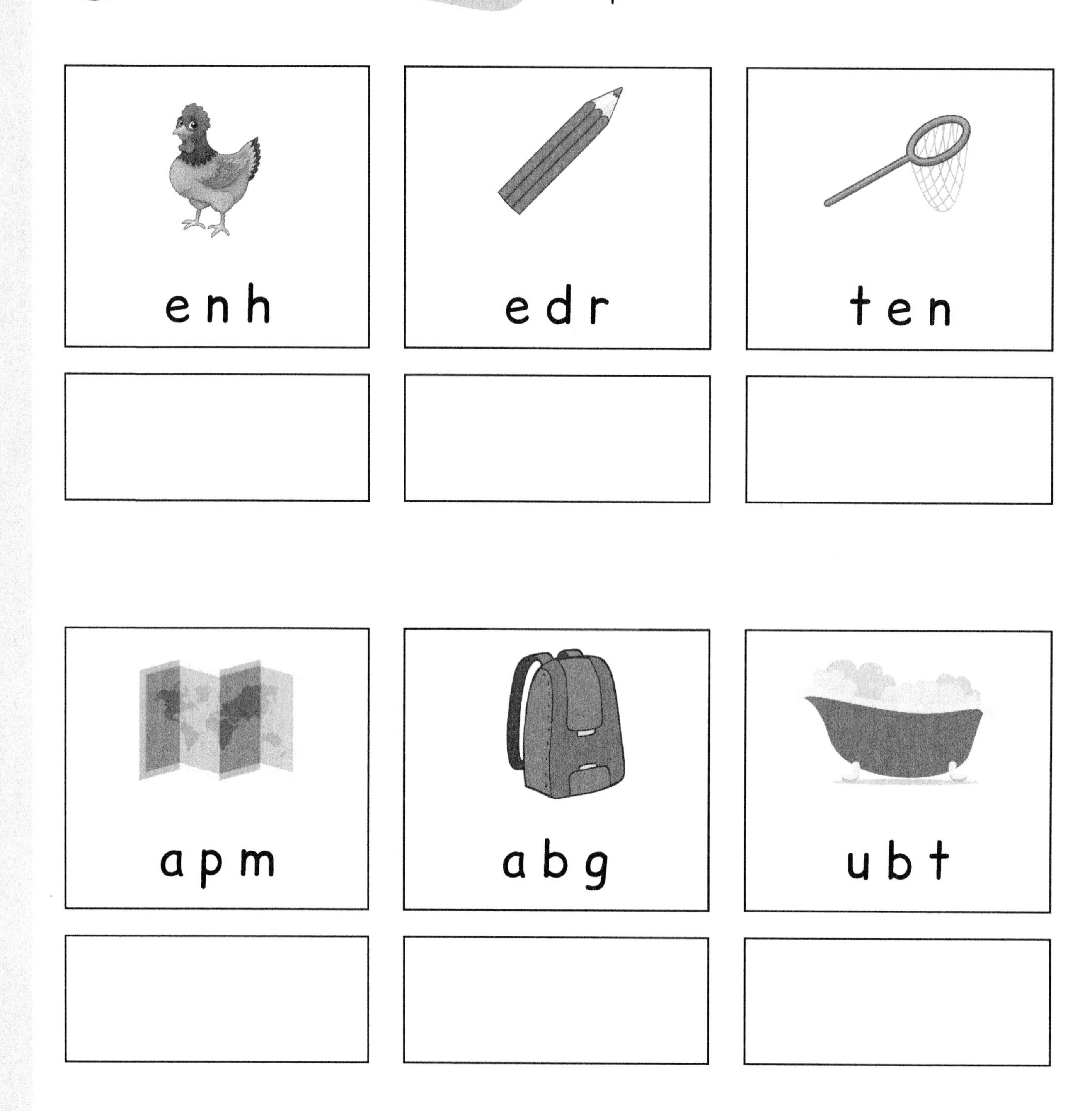

Draw a line to match the pictures with the correct cvc words.

bib

bun

peg

cab

cap

CVC WORDS

Look at the pictures. Write their names below the pictures.

Printed in Great Britain
by Amazon